Container Gardening

A *Sunset* Outdoor Design & Build Guide

By Hank Jenkins and the Editors of *Sunset*

Sunset

©2010 by Time Home Entertainment Inc.
135 West 50th Street, New York, NY 10020

ISBN-13: 978-0-376-01427-6
ISBN-10: 0-376-01427-X
Library of Congress Control Number: 2009937370

10 9 8 7 6 5 4 3 2 1
First Printing December 2010. Printed in the United States of America

OXMOOR HOUSE
VP, PUBLISHING DIRECTOR: Jim Childs
EDITORIAL DIRECTOR: Susan Payne Dobbs
BRAND MANAGER: Fonda Hitchcock
MANAGING EDITOR: Laurie S. Herr

SUNSET PUBLISHING
PRESIDENT: Barb Newton
VP, EDITOR-IN-CHIEF: Katie Tamony
CREATIVE DIRECTOR: Mia Daminato

Outdoor Design & Build Guide: *Container Gardening*
CONTRIBUTORS
AUTHOR: Hank Jenkins
MANAGING EDITOR: Bonnie Monte
ART DIRECTOR: Tracy Sunrize Johnson
PHOTO EDITOR: Philippine Scali
PRODUCTION SPECIALIST: Linda M. Bouchard
COPY EDITOR: Laura Bueno
PROOFREADER: Denise Griffiths
INDEXER: Mary Pelletier-Hunyadi
SERIES DESIGN: Susan Scandrett

To order additional publications, call 1-800-765-6400
For more books to enrich your life, visit **oxmoorhouse.com**
Visit Sunset online at **sunset.com**
For the most comprehensive selection of Sunset books, visit **sunsetbooks.com**
For more exciting home and garden ideas, visit **myhomeideas.com**

FRONT COVER: Photographs by Thomas J. Story

About the Author
Hank Jenkins is a landscape designer and garden speaker specializing in architectural planting and container garden design. He is the owner of Lushland Design, based in Berkeley, California; www.lushlanddesign.com.

Special Thanks
Brett Bachtle; Ruth Bancroft Garden; Leigh Beisch; Kathy Brenzel; Novella Carpenter of Ghost Town Farm; Catherine Chang Design Studio; Jared Crawford of Altar Ecos; Jason Dewees of The Palm Broker; The Dry Garden; East Bay Nursery; Diana Maire Fast; Flora Grubb Gardens; Flowerland, Albany, CA; Sean Franzen; Mark Hawkins; Trish Jenkins; Stephanie Johnson; Laura Martin, Brianne McElhiney; Simon Mowbray; Kimberley Navabpour; Marie Pence; Linda Lamb Peters; Alan Phinney; Amy Quach; Lorraine Reno; Vanessa Speckman; E. Spencer Toy; Michael Weston

contents

Inspiration

Designing Your Container

Pots come in all styles, sizes, and materials. Choose the perfect one for your situation, then select plants that complement one another and the container. Work with form, color, texture, and scale to bring it all together into a beautiful composition.

Projects

A step-by-step primer on planting a container garden, plus 28 projects to suit all situations and styles. Grow edibles, aquatics, succulents, hanging plants, and much more. Includes plant lists, planting diagrams, and information about soil, sun, watering, and fertilizing.

Culture and Care

How to care for your container garden to keep it healthy and lush for many seasons. Expert advice on tools, watering, fertilizing, repotting, pruning, and combating pests and diseases.

Finishing the Look

Tips on grouping and placement show you how to display your container garden for maximum impact. Plus, ideas for all the places to use a container garden to light up a space: rooftops, patios, entryways, and more.

Inspiration

Think of containers as problem-solvers. Short on space to work with? No time to maintain an entire garden? Want to grow plants that need special conditions? Containers to the rescue. They offer a manageable way to enjoy all the beauty and benefits of your own personal garden, whether it be on a balcony, patio, rooftop, windowsill, or wall.

You can grow just about anything in a container, from plants that stimulate the senses with aroma and texture to abundant edible gardens. With the proper soil, drainage, exposure, and nourishment, your garden will flower and fruit just as it would in the ground.

In this book, you'll discover awe-inspiring looks that are easy to imitate, the ideas behind the designs, guidelines for composing your own container garden, and tips for keeping your containers thriving, thrilling, and productive.

Transform a so-so spot into something exceptional with a stylish container garden. This collection delivers a mix of vibrant texture and living color.

contemporary

RIGHT: Succulents have become the latest in fashionable flora, and for good reason. Their architectural form makes them bold and beautiful companions for containers.

FACING PAGE: Tillandsias—or air plants—thrive without soil. Just set one in a handsome container for an eye-catching display.

formal

ABOVE: A mix of chartreuse, royal purple, and velvety green spills from an architectural cast-iron urn.

LEFT: Clean lines and a repetition of pots and plants create a formal, tailored look.

FACING PAGE: The vibrant colors and relaxed forms of violet *Scaevola* and chartreuse *Lysimachia nummularia* 'Aurea' offer a pleasing contrast to the urn's aristocratic profile and rusty patina.

informal

LEFT: Deep violet leaves of *Colocasia esculenta* 'Black Magic' stand tall as *Nymphaea* water lilies float like serene sculptures just above the water's reflective surface. The contrasting forms produce an engaging moment in the stillness of this water garden.

ABOVE: A *Pelargonium* sprawls unchecked over the rim of a formal urn, creating whimsy and playfulness.

11

edible

LEFT: Containers provide a convenient way to grow your own produce easily and organically.

BELOW LEFT: Fragrant, flavorful herbs don't require much room and can thrive in containers. Using herb starts rather than seeds is a great way to get a jump on a productive edible garden.

FACING PAGE: Put fresh fruit at your fingertips. Many varieties, like dwarf citrus, thrive in large containers.

BELOW RIGHT: Besides being a delicious addition to the menu, this leafy kale adds rich texture and color to the landscape.

ABOVE: *Echeveria* 'Afterglow' electrifies with a splash of color and graphic form. It's the perfect complement to the smooth texture and shape of its concrete container.

FACING PAGE: The plants in this artful display echo the colors and textures of the containers, resulting in a stunning composition.

shade

LEFT: Foliage is the star in this vibrant tapestry. The pleated leaves of *Viburnum davidii* mingle with the delicate texture of a red laceleaf *Acer palmatum* Japanese maple, while the new growth of *Pieris japonica* 'Mountain Fire' blazes with color.

RIGHT: The delicate demeanor of these ferns is the perfect foil for the glamour of glass.

ABOVE: These pincushion plants *(Nertera granadensis)* with their abundance of tiny orange berries are playfully paired with gourd containers to create the festive feel of autumn.

FAR LEFT: The frosty glow of *Senecio cineraria* surrounded by icy blue tumbled glass in white glazed containers conjures a wintry landscape.

LEFT: With its profuse blooms that exude an intoxicating vanilla fragrance, *Heliotropium arborescens* is a summertime favorite.

FACING PAGE: The cheerful blossoms of a flowering plum brighten up an outdoor space and signal the start of spring.

Designing
Your Container

Creating the perfect composition is a matter of pairing a pleasing assortment of plants with a complementary container. In this section, we'll look at both: how to choose a container that suits your space and style, as well as how to combine plants in a way that balances color, texture, shape, and form. It all adds up to a fabulous living work of art.

A mix of succulents with striking structural form creates a colorful tapestry in smooth terra-cotta dish containers.

picking
a pot

An autumn palette of gold and red makes this grouping of glazed pots cohesive.

A world of choices beyond the standard flowerpot awaits you, with containers of all shapes, sizes, and materials. There are really no hard-and-fast rules about what works best. It all depends on the space you're trying to fill and the look you're going for. The good news is that with the right soil and the right drainage, just about any vessel can be transformed into an alluring container.

A SENSE OF PLACE

When selecting a pot, think about where it will go and how it relates to the space it will occupy. Is it intended to enliven a dull area, create privacy, welcome people to your front door? These factors can help you determine the style, color, and size of container to choose.

Take stock of the shapes and colors that compose your outdoor environment. Are there strong vertical elements? Is the background a wood deck or richly colored brick? Think about bringing in colors, finishes, and shapes that work with all of these elements.

Containers offer a creative way to link the interior of your house with the space just outside your door—think of this area as an extension of your home. Choosing containers that relate to the color and texture of the interior can create the illusion of a larger living space.

ABOVE: Contemporary containers add subtle texture and an element of height to a garden wall, creating a sense of intimate enclosure along a pathway.

RIGHT: Tapered slate-colored containers planted with *Pittosporum tenuifolium* 'Marjorie Channon', cotoneaster, red 'Dragon's Blood' sedum, and chartreuse juniper dress up these steps with stylish flair.

The rich smoky tones of two tall containers planted with lush, verdant foliage serve as a portal to the sanctuary of a quiet seating area.

STYLE STATEMENTS

Style is about creating energy, a feeling, a defining moment. Is there an existing context that you want to play up? If not, what sort of character do you want to create? Here's a style cheat-sheet.

SUIT THE CONTAINER TO YOUR STYLE	
DESIRED STYLE	**THE BEST CONTAINER**
Contemporary	Sleek finish, smooth or controlled texture, clear-cut lines, bold color, muted tone, unique geometry
Formal	Smooth finish, simple texture, clean lines, solid color
Informal	Assorted finishes, assorted textures, assorted colors and tones
Classic	Smooth finish, embellished details, subtle color and tone
Rustic	Rough, coarse, or weathered finish and texture, muted color, chunky form

A mixture of bold containers filled with giant bird of paradise, palms, *Agave attenuata*, and other succulents creates a tantalizing tropical oasis on a rooftop.

MATTERS OF SIZE

It's important to choose containers with ample growing room, so think about what you'll be planting. A Japanese maple, for instance, will obviously require more space than a cluster of tulips. But bigger isn't always better. A container that's too large for its contents looks awkward. And too much soil can impede your plant's ability to make use of all the moisture in the pot.

Also, avoid containers that are too small. Confined spaces can constrict roots and stress plants. As the roots grow, nutrients are depleted much faster than they would be in an appropriate-size container, creating the need for more maintenance.

In general, you want to supply your plant with a container that is approximately twice the width of the root ball. This allows for new root growth and supplies a sustainable amount of nutrients to get things growing.

An oversize weathered pot gives this majestic Japanese maple plenty of room to put down roots.

ABOVE LEFT: These pots not only have ample growing room for smaller plants, but also can house a small tree or shrub, like this cheerful azalea.

ABOVE RIGHT: A grouping of small containers is a stylish way to feature shallow-rooted bulbs like these irises.

LEFT: Choosing a large container doesn't mean you have to sacrifice style. This classic Italian terra-cotta pot gives a citrus tree room to grow and fruit, while its ornamentation serves up classic sophistication.

CONTAINER SHAPES

Again, think about what you'll be growing. Does the pot's shape support and physically anchor your plants? Shallow-rooted plants can thrive in a shallow container, whereas those that develop extensive root systems or long taproots (the center from which other roots sprout laterally) require a deeper pot. If you'll be growing very tall, top-heavy plants, choose a container that's wide enough at the base to resist toppling over.

Also consider the aesthetics of the various container shapes. Each profile has its design strengths, as explained on the facing page. And suit the shape of your container to the space where it will reside, making sure you can pass by easily without bumping into it.

EFFECTIVE COMBINATIONS OF FORM

CONTAINER	PLANT
Tall	Rounded, arching, vertical
Rectangular	Rounded, arching, cascading
Round	Rounded, arching, vertical, cascading
Square	Rounded, vertical
Flat/Dish	Rounded, vertical, cascading
Tapered	Rounded, arching, vertical, cascading

The antique profile and finish of these containers create an attractive Mediterranean ambience. Their oval profile animates the flat surface behind them with smooth lines that evoke a relaxed feeling.

Tall

» Narrow forms fit nicely into small spaces.

» Strong vertical lines play off similar forms nearby, such as a trellis or a building.

» Elevates plants that might otherwise be overlooked.

» Offers a sleek, contemporary look.

» Brings a sense of energy to a grouping of lower containers.

Rectangular

» Horizontal lines create a sense of movement in a space.

» Establishes order by creating boundaries and borders.

» Looks best when plants are arranged symmetrically.

» Works well in a formal setting.

Round or Egg-Shaped

» Lends a natural, organic feel.

» Has an anchoring effect with a look of stability.

» Creates a sense of volume and circulation when positioned in a central location.

» Shape is enhanced when plants cascade over the edges.

Square

» Presents a balanced and formal structure, yet can also feel contemporary.

» Places emphasis on contents.

» Pairs well with cactus, palms, standard trees, and single-specimen plantings.

» Creates an edgy look when combined with sharp-angled plants.

Flat/Dish

» Excellent for observing from above or in profile.

» Perfect for displaying succulents, bulbs, or mounding alpine plants.

» Useful for elevating plants on a pedestal, or hanging them in staggered groups.

» Offers the perfect platform for cascading or spiller plants.

Tapered

» Evokes a sense of nostalgia as the traditional flowerpot form.

» Tends to direct the eye upward to the expanding foliage of the plants above its rim.

» Can take on a bold, rustic look or a glamorous contemporary feel, thanks to a variety of fresh new designs, glazes, and finishes.

MATERIALS

You'll find containers in a variety of materials, each suited to different situations, since they vary in weight, durability, and how well they hold up to the elements.

Each material has a distinctive look, too, lending personality to a space and setting a tone. So when choosing your container, consider where it will be positioned and the ambience you want to achieve.

care tips

» If you live in a severe climate, you'll need to protect pots that aren't frost-resistant in winter. If they're easy to move, place them against walls that receive warm winter sun or beneath eaves or awnings. Or bring them indoors.

» If you can't move a container to a protected spot, wrap it with burlap or bubble wrap and secure with jute or string. For extra insulation, add a thick layer of straw in between the container and the wrap.

Terra-Cotta

This porous material provides proper drainage and air circulation, but it also allows soil to dry out quickly. Coating terra-cotta containers with a pot sealer will reduce moisture loss.

You can find inexpensive, massed-produced terra-cotta planters as well as more durable high-fired versions. However, all terra-cotta can chip or crack. These containers are heavy, but the benefit is that they are very stable, making them useful for large-specimen trees and shrubs.

Terra-cotta spans shades from pale whitewash to rich earthy reds. Exposed to the elements, the finish can age beautifully. These planters, however, are not frost-proof unless the label indicates so. They hold up in mild-winter climates, but elsewhere it's best to move them indoors for protection until warm weather returns.

DURABILITY: Moderate
FROST RESISTANCE: Low
WATER RETENTION: Low
WEIGHT: Heavy

Vietnamese Black Clay

In recent years, this high-fired material has become an attractive alternative to terra-cotta. One of the hardest clays available, it's also frost-proof and watertight.

DURABILITY: **High**
FROST RESISTANCE: **High**
WATER RETENTION: **High**
WEIGHT: **Heavy**

Glazed Ceramic

Available in a variety of styles, textures, and finishes (glossy or matte), glazed ceramic containers are handy for matching the colors of your home's interior and your exterior landscape. Keep in mind that they're not frost-proof and should be handled carefully to prevent chipping.

DURABILITY: **Moderate**
FROST RESISTANCE: **Low**
WATER RETENTION: **High**
WEIGHT: **Moderate**

Metal

If you want a sophisticated or modern look, metal containers deliver. Copper containers give off a rich charm, iron and steel provide an edgy industrial feel, and zinc is smooth and sophisticated. Note that metal containers, which are heavy, need to be handled carefully as they can scratch and dent easily. If the finish gets nicked, the metal underneath can rust.

You'll find metal containers with three type of finishes: Galvanized metal has a rust-resistant zinc coating. Powder-coated planters have a hard finish of electrostatically applied paint. Polished containers are buffed to create a smooth, bright finish.

DURABILITY: **Moderate**
FROST RESISTANCE: **High**
WATER RETENTION: **High**
WEIGHT: **Heavy**

Wood

Wood containers offer an organic option for the natural insulation of roots and soil. They're also frost-proof. Untreated wood containers are porous and provide ample drainage; treated wood containers are not porous. Keep in mind that treated wood contains toxic chemicals and should not be used for planters that will have edibles growing in them. Redwood, cedar, and cypress are good choices because they resist rot. For an eco-friendly approach, use containers made from reclaimed wood or woodlike renewable resources such as bamboo.

DURABILITY: **Moderate**
FROST RESISTANCE: **High**
WATER RETENTION: **Low**
WEIGHT: **Moderate**

Stone

Stone containers, whether textured or smooth, add a touch of sculpture to any garden. Although they can be very heavy (and expensive), they make a solid design statement. They're also frost-proof. Containers made of stone-and-fiberglass mixtures offer a similar look that is less costly and lighter in weight.

DURABILITY: High
FROST RESISTANCE: High
WATER RETENTION: Moderate
WEIGHT: Heavy

Hypertufa

Made from a mixture of stone aggregate and portland cement, this option resembles stone but is much lighter. And it will stand up to harsh weather conditions.

DURABILITY: Moderate
FROST RESISTANCE: Moderate
WATER RETENTION: Moderate
WEIGHT: Light to Moderate

Synthetic

Faux metal, made of nontoxic, lightweight materials, is gaining in popularity for containers because they're usually less expensive than actual metal ones. They're also frost-proof, rust-proof, UV-resistant, and available in a variety of finishes. They're ideal when you need lightweight, durable containers, such as for a rooftop or balcony.

Another synthetic planter that is quickly becoming a best seller is the soft-sided Woolly Pocket. These flexible, breathable containers are made of recycled plastic bottles and are useful for planting a vertical garden (see the project on page 126).

DURABILITY: **Moderate**
FROST RESISTANCE: **High**
WATER RETENTION: **High**
WEIGHT: **Light**

Found Vessels

For a unique container option, search thrift shops, salvage yards, flea markets, or yard and estate sales. Household objects, recycled goods, and used equipment can take the everyday container garden and turn it into an objet d'art.

Pots with glossy, cool tones create a festive contrast with the vibrant tiled wall that serves as a backdrop.

drainage

P roper drainage is crucial for the health of your plants. Without it, water builds up and either drowns healthy plant roots or fosters soil-borne diseases. Be sure to use an appropriate soil mix (see page 67) and a container with an adequate drainage hole. If your container lacks a hole for drainage, the facing page shows how to add one.

How to Drill Drain Holes in Terra-Cotta, Ceramic, Concrete, or Clay Containers

Place a flat piece of cardboard on a flat, stable surface. Place your overturned container on top of the cardboard. Cardboard provides some stability to your container and reduces vibration.

Take two strips of masking tape and place an "X" over the spot you want to drill.

Before you drill, pour a small pool of water over the spot to be drilled. This provides lubrication and helps reduce heat that could crack or shatter your container.

Wearing protective eyewear, use the small drill bit to create a starter or pilot hole in the center of your "X." This provides a guide hole for your bit and keeps it from jumping around when you drill.

Outfit your drill with the larger bit. Place it over the starter hole. At a slow and steady speed, firmly press your drill down. Drill through the container with a smooth motion.

There may be some slight chipping. Simply dust or wash it off.

If your container is large, add more drainage holes as needed.

WHAT YOU'LL NEED

Cardboard

Masking tape

Protective eyewear

Drill

For terra-cotta, ceramic, concrete, or clay: ³⁄₁₆" **and** 1" **masonry, ceramic, or diamond core drill bits**

For metal: ³⁄₁₆" **and** 1" **metal drill bits**

How to Drill Drain Holes in Metal and Wood Containers

Place a flat piece of cardboard on a flat, stable surface. Place your overturned container on top of the cardboard.

Mark the spot you want to drill with a pencil or marker.

Wearing protective eyewear, use the small drill bit to create a starter hole.

Outfit your drill with the larger metal drill bit. Pressing straight down on your starter hole, drill all the way through in a smooth and steady motion.

Remove any splinters or metal shavings.

In many cases, metal containers require several drain holes to increase air circulation. Because metal holds heat, boosting air flow helps keep roots from scorching on hot days.

care tip

» Elevating pots off the ground encourages good drainage, provides ample air circulation, and protects surfaces from water stains. If you're using a saucer under your container, raise the saucer off the ground and also elevate the container within the saucer. Doing so speeds the evaporation of any runoff that would otherwise stagnate.

Pot feet work well for lifting plants, as do bricks, wood blocks, flat stones, and overturned empty containers. Wood risers on wheels provide the added benefit of mobility. Down Under Plant Stands (see "Resource Guide," page 184) can be adjusted to fit under any size pot.

When Drain Holes Aren't an Option

If you have a container with zero drainage and no means of adding any—say, a glass vessel—you can still plant. Just be sure to water lightly and let soil dry between each watering. Invest in a moisture gauge (available at most nurseries), or use a chopstick to probe the soil.

The key is vigilance. Be on alert for foul odors that may signal water collection, stagnation, and the presence of disease. Or set a smaller pot that does have drainage into the solid vessel. Be sure to add some gravel under the smaller pot to keep it from sitting in water that runs out the bottom. If you're able, periodically empty water that collects in the larger pot.

selecting plants

Grouping a bunch of tasty herbs that can grow well together, such as these starts, can provide you with a bounty of flavor. Plant them in a container close to your back door for instant access to home-grown seasoning.

The plants that end up together in your container will be cohabiting in close quarters, so be sure they have similar requirements when it comes to water and sun.

Beyond that, have fun creating combinations that delight the senses, keeping in mind the basic design principles on the following pages.

DESIGN GUIDELINES

Strive for a Visual Balance in Your Composition

Look at colors, shapes, and textures. Do they look like they belong together or relate to one another? If it seems like you have too much of one thing, reduce the quantity or pull it out all together.

Consider Scale

How does the size of each plant relate to the size of the container and the size of the other plants? Trust your eye. If something appears out of balance with the surrounding composition, it is probably out of scale. If you are able to carry your container around with you at the nursery, you can immediately see what works.

Choose a Star

When building your composition, try giving one plant the lead role and let the others act as the supporting cast.

Work with Only Three Different Forms and Colors of Plants

Combining too many forms and colors leads to an overly busy composition. Using a more limited plant palette can create a surprisingly powerful container garden. As you train your eye to see what works, you can expand on the quantity and variety.

Cast a Critical Eye

Does your composition feel complete? Are you satisfied with the look? If not, edit your selections.

Orange chrysanthemum blossoms and cream variegated foliage blend together into a symphony of color that complements this gold container.

A trained rhododendron in abundant bloom takes center stage in this container setting. Supporting plants help to balance the composition and emphasize the star of the show.

Graduated sizes and unified colors give this trio of hanging pots a visual punch.

YOUR PLANT PALETTE

Plants are the ingredients that add flavor and spice to your design recipe. Consider these six factors when choosing your palette: foliage, flower, color, texture, silhouette, and structure. Understanding how these elements work individually and together will help you design container gardens that can beautifully alter the dynamics of a space. Want to create a sense of depth in a small alcove? Add a layer of richness? Set a particular mood? Let the principles on the following pages guide the way as you select plants that achieve your goal.

Foliage is what clothes plants, and it can dress up a container garden. Here a medley of begonia leaves offers a kaleidoscope of color, form, and texture.

Foliage

Although flowers might be the first feature that comes to mind when you're considering plants, they should actually be secondary. It's the foliage that's the key to a successful container garden design. That's because foliage is almost always present, no matter what the season. Flowers, on the other hand, can come and go. Their presence is an added bonus. A well-designed container garden should be able to stand on its own without flowers.

The effect of foliage depends on its size, shape, and texture. Trying for a wild, lush look? Use big, broad foliage. It provides scale and creates atmosphere, serving as that "wow" factor. Smaller foliage is great for emphasizing the forms around it, whether it's other plants, a garden structure, or a building's architecture. It's the perfect foil for larger foliage. By mixing small and large foliage, you can create a sense of layering as well as an illusion of space.

Think about leaf shape too. Shape can be used to link plants or to add contrast.

Round
Calming, restful

Spiky
Energetic, emphatic, contrasting

Fernlike
Energetic, emphatic, contrasting

Palmate
Exotic, dramatic, bold

Grassy
Soft, flowing, kinetic

Pinnate (featherlike)
Delicate, primal

The bright orange blaze of these dahlia blossoms invites you to visually bask in their cheerful glow.

Flowers

Flowers are the light show of the garden, the beacons of color. They have the ability to grab attention immediately with color, form, and visual texture. As a result, they tend to bring the whole garden into focus. Less showy flowers can have the reverse effect by making plants appear to fade into the background, which creates a sense of spaciousness.

Color

Color is emotional and evokes distinct moods. When looking to plants for color, consider their value—hot, neutral, or cool.

Hot, or vibrant, colors create a strong reaction, grabbing your attention. They jump out, making things appear closer than they are. Using hot-colored plants toward the back of a composition can make plants in the foreground pop. Use hot colors in moderation. Overabundance can create an anxious mood.

Cool colors are at the opposite end of the spectrum. They have a calming, restful effect and create a sense of distance and depth. They're great for toning down hot colors. The contrast of pairing cool and hot colors—such as deep purple with silver—brings energy to a plant palette.

Neutral colors provide a balance, softening hot colors and intensifying cool colors.

COLOR PROFILE		
VALUE	COLOR	MOOD
Hot	Red	Vibrant
Hot	Orange	Inviting
Hot	Yellow	Stimulating
Hot	White	Luminous
Hot	Silver	Galvanizing
Neutral	Green	Balancing
Neutral	Brown	Comforting
Cool	Blue	Calming
Cool	Purple	Luxurious

Combining Color

Don't let the prospect of mixing and matching color intimidate you! It's an opportunity to let the designer inside you shine. Look at colors in your home, in nature, and in the clothing you wear. Think about how those colors make you feel. When you see an interesting combination, what draws you toward it? Do the colors relate or contrast in an interesting way? Now take what you like about color and apply it to plants that you find appealing. As you experiment, you'll be able to see what works and what doesn't. Here are a few suggestions to get you started.

For a relaxed, harmonious look, try pairing analogous colors, which are next to each other on a color wheel. For example, different tones of yellow with varied tones of green can result in a look that is restful. But the combination also gives you a sense of depth and layering that can make small spaces feel larger. Analogous color combinations provide a subtle yet refreshing energy.

If you're after a more elegant, refined look, try a monochromatic approach. Using one color can set a bold tone and is effective for creating a formal look. Take it a step further by mixing up different shapes of foliage and flower to really add some interest.

For a contemporary look, try using colors that complement each other. Pairing complementary colors—opposite one another on the color wheel—creates a stimulating sense of balance.

RIGHT, TOP TO BOTTOM: The blend of yellow foliage and flower combines with tones of green to produce a pleasant, restful look. A trio of gray tapered containers filled with rich green tropical foliage contrasts elegantly with a matte blue background. Make a statement by experimenting with a bold mixture of colors that share similar tone or intensity.

VIBRANT COLOR COMBINATIONS

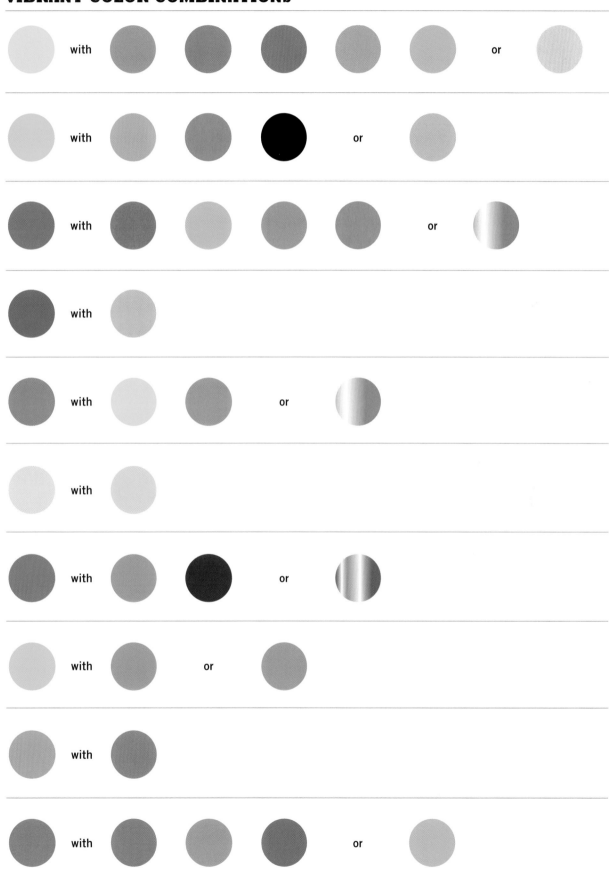

Visual Weight

Another property of color is its strength, or visual weight—the degree to which it catches the eye. When it comes to plants, visual weight can be described as high, medium, or low. The higher the visual weight or brighter the color, the quicker it captures your attention.

HIGH VISUAL WEIGHT. These are the colors that create drama and grab you first. Use them to energize a composition or establish focal points.

MEDIUM VISUAL WEIGHT. These colors create a sense of volume and flow. They help balance high and low visual weights.

LOW VISUAL WEIGHT. Colors of this weight can tone down intensity and provide a subtle richness. For a relaxed look, concentrate on colors with a low visual weight.

LOW VISUAL WEIGHT

design tips

》 The greater the contrast in color, the more it emphasizes each plant's form. But too much contrast can result in a chaotic, unsettling look.

》 Avoid dark color contrasts in shady situations. They won't read.

TOP: The pastel blues and purples of forget-me-nots possess a low visual weight that creates a soft, subtle look.

BOTTOM: The medium visual weight of an earthy, bronze container garnished by the green lobed leaves of the *Grevillea* 'Poorinda Blondie' is soothing.

MEDIUM VISUAL WEIGHT

The fiery red fall foliage of a Japanese maple exhibits a high visual weight as it ignites interest and immediately catches the eye.

HIGH VISUAL WEIGHT

Boxleaf honeysuckle (*Lonicera nitida*), golden Japanese sweet flag (*Acorus gramineus* 'Ogon'), *Leucothoe*, and *Skimmia* produce a luminous composition in a cobalt container.

The Effect of Light

Keep in mind that plant color can change at different times of the day and in different light. The same container garden placed in full sunlight might take on a completely different look in a shadier spot.

Hot colors benefit from lots of light. Yellow, for example—with its bright, uplifting qualities—becomes even more vibrant in full sunlight. Reds become spicier, silvers shimmer, and golds glimmer. This vibrancy can increase the richness of your container garden. Some hot colors are effective in low light too. White,

for instance, can really put on a show when viewed in clear moonlight, where it takes on an ethereal quality. Silvers provide a glint of color that can be intoxicating

Cool colors come alive in low light. Blue, for instance, is one of the last colors to fade as daylight turns to night. It can have a quieting effect at the end of a day that was filled with bright, riotous light.

Two light-colored containers illuminate a dark seating area with lush green growth featuring spotlights of bright white foliage and flower.

A container glazed in sea green holds *Pennisetum setaceum* 'Red Riding Hood', whose soft seed heads shimmer as they catch the light.

Texture

Utilizing texture can amp up the three-dimensional aspect of your container garden. Texture is all about the appearance or feel of a surface—whether it's the surface of a plant, a container, or both.

Texture can be glossy, matte, or fuzzy. It can take on a structural quality by appearing spiky, feathery, or waxy. Also consider the degree of texture. Fine texture is usually small and subtle, best viewed up close. Visually it creates a light, airy, relaxing, soft look. Coarse texture is eye-catching and bold. Visually it provides contrast to other materials and can be seen from a distance. Medium-textured plants fall somewhere in between or exhibit a combination of coarse and fine.

Flowers add as much texture as they do color. Here they range from paperlike to velvety in this group of primroses, pansies, anemones, and violas.

The bold texture of agave rosettes and the broad tropical leaves of giant bird of paradise create exciting visual volume that brings surrounding surfaces to life.

TOP: The fine-textured leaves of a maidenhair fern have a delicately soft, cloudlike appearance as they float above a sky blue bowl.

BOTTOM: *Agave macrantha's* spiky blue foliage tipped in purplish black spines displays a coarse, forceful texture that adds excitement and energy.

A lush mixture of succulent and tropical foliage artfully combines fine and coarse textures.

Using Texture

There's more to texture than just the way it feels. Light reflecting off the textured surface of a pot or a plant adds a sense of richness and depth. Some plant surfaces also capture moisture, causing water to bead up and create a dewy look, reminiscent of a rain forest. Use these textural properties to enhance your container garden.

Fine-Textured Plants

Using fine-textured plants—with their small leaves and tightly growing stems—is a good way to create a sense of "background." They tend to play the subordinate role to coarser, bolder plants by bringing out their color, form, and the spaces between their leaves. Fine-textured plants have a soft, delicate look that entices people to get closer, reach out, and touch.

Coarse-Textured Plants

To grab attention, consider coarse-textured plants, which tend to have large leaves, thick stems, and a bold, graphic look. They're great at contrasting light and shadow as well as providing a sense of energy. Their substantial look allows them to stand solo without flowers. With such a prominent presence, they are perfect for anchoring a container garden as well as giving you a starting point when you plant.

Combining Textures

Mixing textures is the secret to creating stylish containers. This technique is especially useful for containers intended for small spaces, where you really notice texture up close. Aim to create a balance between fine and coarse textures. Their individual attributes can be combined for amazing visual effects that take a container garden beyond its reliance on color.

The soft, fine texture of Australian astro-turf, the laciness of maidenhair fern, and the chunky coarseness of English primrose foliage add up to a pleasing visual balance.

The intriguing pinwheel-like form of *Aeonium* 'Zwartkop', effervescent thyme, and spilling 'Dragon's Blood' sedum bring structural variety to this arrangement.

Silhouette and Structure

Another principle to include in your palette is silhouette, created by a plant's outline. Unusual branching patterns or a weeping form add impact to your container garden. Deciduous plants can have distinctive silhouettes both in and out of leaf, providing year-round interest. Boldly shaped flower clusters—such as those of agave or bird of paradise—are another way to work a strong silhouette into a design.

Try featuring a plant with a striking silhouette in a container where it can stand alone and show off without the interference of surrounding plants. Place your container near or against a wall that can serve as a backdrop.

Structure is closely related to silhouette, but it refers to the shape of all the plant's parts, not just its outline—the details of foliage, stem, and flower combined. As you select plants, take a moment to observe their overall structure, which provides clues about how to best use them in your composition.

Different plant forms, or structure, can have different effects in a composition. Horizontal forms give a sense of space. Vertical forms can provide direction or create a focal point. Neutral forms add bulk to a composition. If you don't see the structure you want in a plant, fine-tune it by simply pruning. Just make sure your plant is amenable to pruning.

Experiment to create combinations of silhouette and structure that are pleasing to your eye. The more you work with these elements, the more you'll gain an understanding of what is successful and what is not.

The red whiplike stems of a red-twig dogwood provide a scintillating silhouette in a container during the dull winter months.

This container planting is big on structure, thanks to the aloe's swirling, swordlike structure.

putting form
to use

Boost excitement by using upright, directional plant forms in your container garden to attract the eye and hold attention.

To create a dynamic composition in your container, combine plants that exhibit different forms. There are four basic forms that plants can take: upright/directional, round/non-directional, arching/spreading, and cascading/ground-covering/trailing. The following pages describe the different forms.

THE THRILL OF IT ALL: UPRIGHT/DIRECTIONAL FORM

The lead role in your container garden is usually best played by an upright or directional plant. These plants create an emphasis on all things vertical, punctuating an otherwise ordinary grouping of softer, relaxed shapes by providing contrast.

Vertical elements attract and hold attention briefly before your eye moves on. They create an air of narrowness or slenderness. By their extension, they exude a sense of robustness, vigor, and growth. Containers with strong vertical elements offer a captivating way to mark an entrance or exit. They also have the ability to direct attention, whether it's up above, down below, or right in front of you.

Limit the number of upright or directional plants in a container garden. Too many can confuse and clutter your composition.

ABOVE: Both the phormium in the large container, with foliage resembling flickering flames, and the *Libertia peregrinans* in the smaller container behave like visual exclamation points.

RIGHT: The formal stature of well-clipped foliage atop vertically trained trunks is accented with a frill of fuzzy grass.

FLAVORFUL FILLINGS: ROUND/NON-DIRECTIONAL FORM

Rounded forms are an ideal platform from which vertical and arching forms can rise. Although monotonous when used alone, they are the perfect companions to other forms, establishing a soft, neutral setting that anchors the other plants in your container garden. They create symmetry and complement asymmetry by providing balancing chunks of volume. These forms will most likely represent the majority of the plants in your composition, creating a surface texture that contributes to a layered look.

ABOVE: The rounded form created by the arching stems of *Plectranthus* 'Heigh-Ho Silver' provides a counterpoint to the vertical aspect of Australian silver rush (*Juncus polyanthemos*).

RIGHT: These clipped rounded boxwood shrubs balance the angular lines of a balcony border. Spilling *Helichrysum petiolare* further softens the look.

The mounding, rounded form of Atlas fescue *(Festuca mairei)* creates a neutral backdrop that both complements and showcases the cascading character of *Tradescantia* 'Baby Bunny Bellies'.

THE SPACE IN BETWEEN: ARCHING/SPREADING FORM

These forms are similar to rounded forms, but they have a looser, more open habit. Their branches, foliage, and stems visually connect other plants in a composition by reaching out, across, and over them. The result is a sense of visual rhythm and flow as their form extends through—and in some cases beyond—your composition.

This unifying effect can either energize or relax a composition. For example, spiky, upright arching foliage emits a sense of energy, whereas lazy, languid stems produce a leisurely, unhurried effect.

BELOW LEFT: The dark, arching blades of fountain grass add a playful presence and colorful contrast to the yellow pansies.

BELOW: The bold strap-leaf foliage of a phormium creates a stylish rhythm as it elegantly erupts and flows between heuchera and heather.

design tip

» Choose arching/spreading plants that have an open habit so the plants they cross over can be seen.

The arching foliage of lemongrass reaches out and over to neighboring herbs and vegetables. Its form helps connect this grouping of edible container gardens.

Dichondra argentea 'Silver Falls' spills like liquid silver over the edges of an antique urn. The waterfall effect is luminous and luxurious.

BUILT TO SPILL:
CASCADING/GROUND-COVERING/TRAILING

These plants hug the soil and creep horizontally. Use them as a finishing touch in your compositions to fill in any gaps between other plants. They also provide a great counterbalance to plants with upright or directional form.

Some can remain rigidly horizontal while other relaxed forms can cascade over the edge of a container like a waterfall, producing a soft, soothing effect. These plants can also be used as ribbons of color or texture running through and beyond a composition. This same effect can conjure up feelings of wildness as stems escape the confines of your container rim. For a more graphic look, try using tight ground-covering forms that will take on the shape of the soil surface in your container as they grow.

As cascading, ground-covering, trailing plants get older, they might develop gaps in growth. To get things looking lush again, you can cut back to renew growth or simply remove the old plant and replace it.

Parrot's Beak *(Lotus berthelotii)*, with its soft needlelike foliage and flaming flowers, creates a sensation as it spills over the edges of gleaming cylindrical containers.

The trailing stems of two colors of *Lysimachia nummularia* balance a planting of pheasant's-tail grass *(Anemanthele lessoniana)*, rusty orange coleus, and blue-green *Euphorbia polychroma*.

Projects

You've got your container and your plants. Now it's time to turn on your creativity. In this section, we'll show you some ideas for transforming an empty container into a captivating composition. The 28 designs featured here provide every detail you'll need: materials, suggested plants, project tips, and the basics of how to build something beautiful. Let these projects help cultivate new ideas, inspire your creativity, and offer stylish solutions.

Grab some gardening gear, gather your plants and your pot, and start creating your composition.

getting started

Nutrient-rich,
well-draining soil
gives your plants
a healthy foundation.

To ensure adequate drainage and all the essential nutrients, it's best to use either a pre-made, high-quality potting soil or mix your own. Topsoil dug straight out of the garden is not a good idea. It can harbor disease, and it may be too dense to provide proper drainage.

THE DIRT ON SOIL

Most ready-made mixes are a blend of composted tree bark, peat moss or coconut coir (made of composted coconut fiber), organic fertilizers, and drainage grit such as pumice or sand. These mixes are light and easy to use.

For plants that have special soil requirements, the following specialty mixes are available at local nurseries.

» **Acid-loving plant mix:** Great for evergreens, ferns, camellias, rhododendrons, fuchsia, and begonias.

» **Aquatic plant mix:** Made from zeolite, a crushed volcanic rock that absorbs nutrients from water and slowly releases it to plant roots. It stays put in containers that are submerged in water and doesn't cloud.

» **Cactus and succulent mix:** This mix is specifically formulated to provide fast drainage.

» **Lightweight soil blends:** This light and fluffy mix is composed primarily of a peat moss or coconut coir base. It's perfect for reducing the weight of containers like hanging baskets and window boxes. Just keep in mind that it tends to dry out quickly.

Making Your Own Soil

Mixing your own soil is easy and gives you control over exactly which nutrients your plant is getting.

BASIC RECIPE

2 parts potting mix or compost, provides micro- and macronutrients

1 part coconut coir, aids in moisture retention

1 to 2 parts coarse sand or horticultural pumice, aids drainage and aeration

1 part well-rotted steer manure, provides micro- and macronutrients

Vary the amount of sand or horticultural pumice to meet the drainage needs of the plants you use.

Soil Polymers

Also known as wetting agents, soil polymers are designed to be mixed with potting soil to provide steady moisture to plant roots. Polymers such as Broadleaf P4 can absorb 100 to 200 times their weight in water. They then release the stored water as needed. Soil polymers are nontoxic and biodegradable.

To use them, sprinkle the dry crystals into water, following package directions, and stir until they swell to form a thick gel. Pour your potting mix into a wheelbarrow or other large container. Then add the gel, following the proportions listed on the package, and combine well. Once the crystals and soil mix are thoroughly combined, fill your pots and start planting.

HOW MUCH SOIL

SOIL QUANTITY	CONTAINERS IT WILL FILL
1½ cubic feet	One 48-inch x 6-inch x 6-inch planter or window box
2 cubic feet	Eight to ten standard 10- to 12-inch containers One 15-gallon container One 36-inch x 8-inch x 10-inch planter or window box
3 cubic feet	Two 36-inch x 6-inch x 6-inch planters or window boxes

Adding compost as well as drainage components, such as horticultural pumice or coarse sand, is a good way to improve a mix's moisture retention, drainage ability, and structure.

HOW TO PLANT A CONTAINER

Now it's time to put together your composition. It's a good idea to try out different arrangements before you actually plant. The easiest way to do that is to partially fill your container with soil and set your plants in while they're still in their nursery pots. That makes it easy to move them around until everything looks just the way you want. When you're satisfied, take a photo or make notes of your arrangement, remove the pots, and start planting.

WHAT YOU'LL NEED

Container with drain hole

Drainage screen

Potting mix

Trowel or scoop

Plants

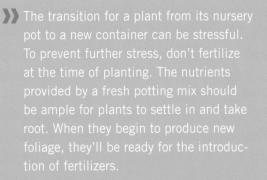

care tip

›› The transition for a plant from its nursery pot to a new container can be stressful. To prevent further stress, don't fertilize at the time of planting. The nutrients provided by a fresh potting mix should be ample for plants to settle in and take root. When they begin to produce new foliage, they'll be ready for the introduction of fertilizers.

❶ Prepare Your Pot

Make sure the container has an ample drain hole. (If you need to drill a hole, see page 37.) Before adding soil, cover the drain hole with a premade soil-stopper screen or small square of window screen. Don't use potting shards or stones; they can plug up the hole and waterlog the soil.

❷ Loosen the Root Ball

Fill your container three-quarters full with well-draining planting mix. Working with one plant at a time, remove it from the nursery pot by turning it over and giving the sides a few gentle squeezes, then sliding the plant out. Carefully tease the root ball apart. Don't worry about losing some of the soil from the root ball.

❸ Place the Plants

Position the plant in your container, and add soil around it to anchor it. Repeat with the rest of the plants. Position tall plants toward the back or just off-center, and arrange supporting plants around them. Place cascading or spilling plants near the edges.

❹ Add More Soil and Water

Fill in the gaps between your newly placed plants with additional soil. Keep soil level an inch below the lip of your container to reduce soil loss during watering. Make sure all roots are tucked in and plants are stable. Finish by pruning away any dead, damaged, or diseased plant growth as well as spent flowers. Give your plants a good drink of water.

Besides using a fresh potting mix, the other secret to a successful container garden is selecting healthy, vigorous plants. Avoid scraggly plants and those that show signs of pests and disease.

HOW TO PLANT AN AQUATIC POT

A container filled with water-loving plants adds a cool oasis to the landscape and makes a welcome spot for birds to stop on hot days.

    When you purchase your plants, be sure to find out how deep to submerge them. Some prefer that the soil line be at the water's surface, while others need their soil to be entirely underwater. Aquatic plants purchased at a nursery will already be potted in appropriate soil for growing in water, ready to be set directly into your container. Or if they're a free-floating variety, they'll be packed in water.

WHAT YOU'LL NEED

Watertight container

Gravel or stone for creating a base layer in the bottom of the container

Bricks, small pavers, or over-turned empty pots for elevating plants

Aquatic plants in nursery pots

Water

Mosquito dunks or mosquito bits

care tip

» If you can't find zeolite aquatic soil for your water plants, you can use "calcified clay" cat litter. It has the same consistency as zeolite and the same nutrients as clay soil. Just make sure it has not been chemically treated or deodorized.

❶ Prepare Your Pot
Make sure the container is water-tight. If it has a drain hole, plug it with a cork or sealing compound, and seal with waterproof silicone caulk. Another option is to use a durable plastic liner that fits inside your pot. Place your container in a sunny spot. Water plants require lots of light, and once you add water, the container will be too heavy to move.

❷ Add Gravel or Stones
Fill the bottom of your container with gravel or stones to create a level base. Also sprinkle a layer of gravel into each of your potted plants to help keep soil from floating out.

❸ Place Plants
Marginal plants like to be positioned with their soil line just below the water surface. Set them on bricks or overturned pots to elevate them. Deep-water plants can be set up to 12 inches below the surface, either on the stone base or on other elevation material.

❹ Add Water
Fill container with water, up to ½ inch below rim and add a mosquito dunk to control larvae.

» Arrowhead *(Sagittaria latifolia)*
White flower spikes, arching leaves. Submerge pot.

» Canna
Broad waxy leaves and striking gladiola-like flowers. Preferred depth varies depending on the type.

» Dwarf cattail *(Typha minima)*
Narrow blue-green leaves and 1-inch cattails. Submerge pot.

» Dwarf papyrus *(Cyperus isocladus)*
Long narrow leaves and flowers. Submerge pot.

» Horsetail *(Equisetum hyemale)*
Rushlike, joined hollow stems. Submerge pot halfway.

» Japanese iris *(Iris ensata)*
Velvety blooms, sword-shaped leaves. Submerge pot halfway. Remove pot from water during plant's dormant season.

» Lotus *(Nelumbo)*
Showy flowers, big round leaves above water. Submerge pot.

» Umbrella plant *(Cyperus alternifolius)*
Spreading leaves. Submerge pot.

» Variegated striped tush
(*Baumea rubiginosa* 'Variegata')
Stiff, spearlike leaves striped with bright yellow. Submerge pot.

» Water hyacinth *(Eichhornia crassipes)*
Violet flowers, floating leaves. Free-floating.
NOTE: This plant is quite invasive and should not be introduced into natural bodies of water.

» Water lettuce *(Pistia stratiotes)*
Light green lettucelike foliage. Free-floating.

» Water lily *(Nymphaea)*
Showy flowers, round floating leaves. Submerge pot.

Routine Care

Periodically add water to replace what's lost through evaporation, trim plants as needed, and fertilize regularly. About once a year, empty your container and clean it with a solution of 1 part bleach to 4 parts water. Rinse thoroughly before putting plants back in.

Fertilizing

For water plants growing in soil, use aquatic plant food in tablet form. Lift potted plants out of the water, push a tablet firmly into the soil, and return the pot to the container. Avoid liquid fertilizers, which can encourage the growth of algae in your container. Liquid fertilizers are excellent, though, for floating aquatic plants. Transfer free-floaters to a watertight container with liquid fertilizer added according to package directions. Let the plant sit for a day or two, then return it to the container garden.

Controlling Mosquitoes

The problem with standing water is that it's where mosquitoes lay their eggs. To keep the insects from reproducing in your aquatic container, use mosquito bits (granules) or dunks (donut-shaped disks). These products contain a biological control (Bt-israelensis) that kills larvae for up to 30 days but is harmless to wildlife.

Just like plants in soil, your aquatic plants will reward you with a lush display if you give them the sunlight and nutrients they need.

made
in the shade

Capture a romantic moment with the elegant beauty of moss planters brimming with sophisticated shade-loving plants. Let these compositions thrill, spill, and fill a quiet space with vibrant color, texture, and form.

A. Angel's Wing Begonia

(*Begonia* 'Irene Nuss') This cane-type begonia produces bamboo-like stems and is covered in deep green leaves with rich burgundy undersides. Plants can grow 2½ to 5 feet in height, providing a valuable vertical element. From late spring through early autumn, they produce huge drooping clusters of coral-pink flowers.

B. *Fuchsia* 'Autumnale'

This sprawling shrub has radiant gold-green foliage flushed with orange and fuchsia accents. Plants also produce red and purple flowers that are a hummingbird favorite. The shrub grows 6 to 18 inches tall and 18 inches wide.

C. Round-Leaf Fern

(*Pellaea rotundifolia*) A tidy-growing fern with charming round foliage that provides excellent textural contrast to both fine- and large-leafed plants. Grows a foot tall and up to 2 feet wide.

HOW TO GROW IT

EXPOSURE: Filtered sun/shade
WATER: Regular
SOIL: Acid-loving plant mix (commonly sold as Azalea, Camellia, Rhododendron Planting Mix)
FERTILIZER: Slow-release fertilizer in spring or monthly liquid fertilizer spring through fall once plants are established

ABOVE: *Fuchsia* 'Autumnale'

ABOVE RIGHT: Round-leaf fern

RIGHT: Angel's wing begonia

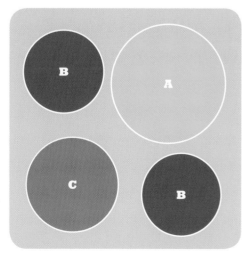

BUILD IT!

Create a stir in a shady spot with a symphony
of color and composition. Bold texture rises from
a bed of variegated and marbled color to create
a beautiful balance that captures the eye and
soothes the soul.

A. *Fatsia japonica* 'Variegata'

Bold, variegated palmate foliage is balanced on long sturdy green stems, giving this shrub a tropical look. Plants can grow 5 to 8 feet tall, providing a distinctive structure to containers. Looks great against a dark background.

B. *Heuchera* 'Snow Angel'

Mound-forming perennial features marbled foliage with light cream variegation. Produces airy stems of tiny pink flowers in spring. Can spread 12 inches wide and produce flower stalks up to 12 inches tall.

C. *Ophiopogon japonicus* 'Pam Harper'

Grasslike perennial with neat, slightly curled leaf blades highlighted with fine-lined creamy white margins. Forms dense clumps from 6 to 8 inches tall. Great filler plant.

D. Mattress Vine

(*Muehlenbeckia complexa*) Vigorously twining vine with thin wiry black or brown stems and small, rounded green foliage. Sprawling form creates a lush cascading look. Can grow 20 to 30 feet in length if left unchecked. Cut back occasionally to control.

HOW TO GROW IT

EXPOSURE: Shade/part sun
WATER: Regular
SOIL: Well-draining planting mix
FERTILIZER: Slow-release fertilizer in spring or monthly liquid fertilizer spring through fall once plants are established

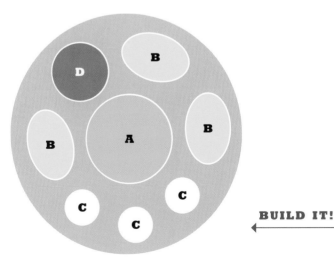

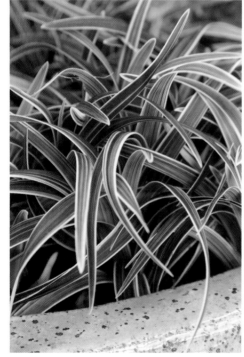

TOP: *Heuchera* 'Snow Angel'   **BOTTOM:** *Ophiopogon japonicus* 'Pam Harper'

BUILD IT! ←

A tapered, glazed container with a stonelike
finish features a fountain of foliage accented
with soft color.

A. Mexican Feather Grass

(Nassella tenuissima) Beautiful, fine-textured ornamental grass. Shimmering, threadlike blades start out green, becoming a soft straw gold as they mature. Plants have an airy, billowing form and can reach 2 feet tall and 2 to 3 feet wide.

B. *Pelargonium* x *hortorum* Daredevil Salmon

Vigorous, bushy geranium that produces long-lasting clusters of bright salmon blossoms all summer. Plants grow 18 to 24 inches tall, adding volume and height to a container.

C. Swan River Daisy

(Brachyscome iberidifolia Blue Zephyr, also sold as 'Mauve Mystique')* Mounding annual Australian daisy with fine-textured, lacy foliage that produces violet-blue daisylike flowers with golden centers. Great filler plant that blooms spring through fall.

D. Bacopa

(Sutera cordata 'Snowstorm Giant Snowflake')* Cascading stemmed creeper with sweet, heart-shaped green leaves that produces continuous blooms of small, golden-throated flowers.

TOP: *Brachyscome iberidifolia* Blue Zephyr

BOTTOM: *Sutera cordata* 'Snowstorm Giant Snowflake'

HOW TO GROW IT

EXPOSURE: Full sun
WATER: Regular
SOIL: Well-draining planting mix
FERTILIZER: Slow-release fertilizer in spring or light feeding of liquid fertilizer every 2 to 4 weeks once plants are established.

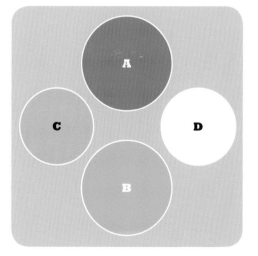

BUILD IT! ←

shades
of green

Lush tones of green and
chartreuse illuminate the
richness of these bronze
containers, while soft
forms cascade gently over
the perimeter.

A. Restio

(Restio multiflorus) A billowy, grasslike plant that grows 3 to 4 feet tall. It develops attractive russet seed heads that provide interest through winter.

B. Native New Zealand Iris

(Libertia peregrinans) Brilliant strappy leaves of orange and olive provide an eye-catching accent. Grows up to 2 feet tall. Produces delicate, white iris-like flowers in late spring through mid-summer.

C. Wood Spurge

(Euphorbia amygdaloides robbiae) This rounded perennial grows up to 1 foot tall and has robust green foliage—the perfect filler.

D. Breath of Heaven

(Coleonema pulchrum 'Sunset Gold') Soft and feathery aromatic foliage gives the arching branches of this plant a delicate character. Growing up to 1½ feet tall, it's the ideal plant for that graceful, overflowing look.

HOW TO GROW IT

EXPOSURE: Full sun
WATER: Regular
SOIL: Well-draining planting mix
FERTILIZER: Slow-release fertilizer in spring or a light feeding of liquid fertilizer every 4 months

Clockwise from top right: Wood spurge, breath of heaven, native New Zealand iris

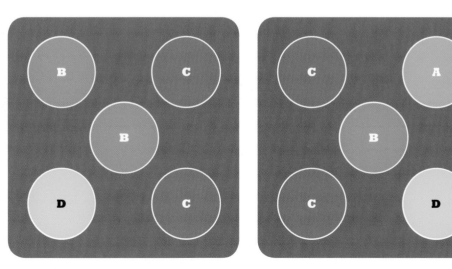

BUILD IT!

The smooth lines of these green tapered containers are crowned in stately style with agave and sedum. The harmonious colors and complementary shapes create a bold sense of excitement.

A. *Agave* 'Cornelius'

This manageable and attractive agave grows only 18 inches tall and dazzles with a rosette of bold lemon-lime variegation. Undulating leaves create a sense of motion and excitement.

B. Golden Sedum

(*Sedum rupestre* 'Angelina') A low-growing, evergreen succulent with vivid lime green and lemon yellow needlelike foliage. Makes for a great groundcover and filler.

Other Agaves for Containers

» *Agave americana* var. *medio-picta alba*

» *Agave attenuata* 'Kara's Stripes'

» *Agave desmettiana* 'Variegata'

» *Agave macroacantha*

» *Agave parryi* var. *truncata*

» *Agave victoriae-reginae*

ABOVE LEFT: *Agave* 'Cornelius'

ABOVE RIGHT: Golden sedum

HOW TO GROW IT

EXPOSURE: Full sun
WATER: Low
SOIL: Cactus mix or fast-draining soil mix
FERTILIZER: 50% diluted or low-concentration all-purpose fertilizer applied once in spring and again in fall

BUILD IT! →

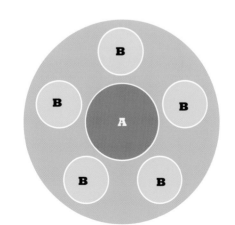

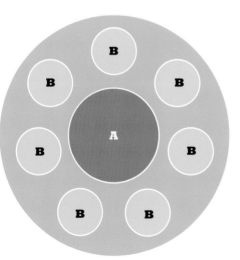

pond
in a pot

Water gardens can create a
serene, relaxed mood. The
stillness of water combined
with plants breaking the
flickering surface brings
a sense of calm.

A. Black Taro

(*Colocasia esculenta* '**Fontanesii**') A tender herbaceous perennial with deep green heart-shaped tropical foliage held aloft by bewitching blackish purple stems. Protect from wind.

B. Little Giant Papyrus

(*Cyperus papyrus* '**Dwarf Form**') Upright, graceful plant with 2- to 3-foot-tall stems topped with soft round bursts of bright green filament-like foliage. Adds drama and height to a container. Protect from wind.

C. Star Grass

(*Dichromena colorata*) Grasslike sedge topped with showy white seed bracts that resemble twinkling stars. Plants grow 12 to 24 inches tall and make good cut flowers. Position in sun or part sun in shallow water.

D. Golden Sweet Flag

(*Acorus gramineus* '**Ogon**') Clumping evergreen, grasslike foliage in striped green with bright yellow is pleasantly aromatic when crushed. Neat 10-inch blades provide both an arching and vertical accent. Place in shallow water.

E. Indian Rhubarb

(*Darmera peltata* '**Umbrella Plant**') Clump-forming perennial produces shield-shaped leaves 1 to 2 feet wide on 2- to 6-foot stalks. In autumn, the foliage takes on brilliant color. Large round clusters of pink blossoms appear in spring before foliage emerges. Keep moist or place in shallow water.

F. Parrot's Feather

(*Myriophyllum brasiliense*) Low-growing water plant produces soft feathery foliage that floats and sprawls on the water's surface. Makes a fine textural element in a water garden. Place in shallow water.

Indian rhubarb

HOW TO GROW IT

EXPOSURE: Full sun
WATER: Aquatic
SOIL: Aquatic plant mix or calcified clay
FERTILIZER: Aquatic plant fertilizer tabs placed in pots once a month during growing season

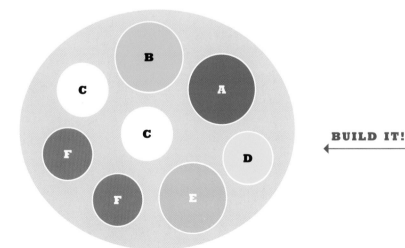

BUILD IT!

Plum and lavender hues punch up an earth-toned container with a lush layered look. Graceful blades grab the eye, while rich color spills over the edge.

A. *Pennisetum purpureum*

Bringing both height and drama to the container setting, the graceful, purple-tinged grass looks good through the growing season. Its color often intensifies with heat. It can grow 60 to 72 inches tall, so start with a 4-inch or 1-gallon container.

B. Summer Snapdragon

(*Angelonia angustifolia* 'Angelface Wedgwood Blue') This upright branching plant grows 18 to 24 inches tall and produces clusters of long-lasting white and lavender flowers from summer through fall. Foliage has a grape essence to it.

C. Bacopa

(*Sutera cordata* 'Cabana Trailing Blue') This 4- to 6-inch-tall trailing plant produces small lavender-blue flowers with golden throats. It is a wonderful filler and spiller plant for containers.

D. *Nemesia fruticans* 'Blue Bird' and 'Safari White'

Mounding plants with sprawling habits that produce an abundant amount of small violet-blue and white flowers dotted with yellow centers. Lightly prune on occasion to encourage repeat blooming. Plants can grow 10 to 12 inches tall and prefer sun or part shade.

E. Supertunia Bordeaux Petunia

Pinkish lavender blooms laced with deep plum-burgundy veins cover this 6- to 10-inch-tall trailing plant summer through autumn. Cut back midsummer for repeat flowering.

F. Dolce Crème de Menthe *Heuchera*

A mounding perennial covered with stunning plum foliage frosted in soft green, giving it the look of stained glass. It can grow 18 to 36 inches tall and wide, tolerating full sun in cool climates, part sun to shade elsewhere.

G. *Carex comans* 'Frosted Curls'

Clumping fine-textured grass with a lazy, weeping habit makes a great spiller with a soft, flowing look. Clump can grow 12 inches tall and trail 2 to 3 feet.

Clockwise from upper right: Supertunia Bordeaux petunia, bacopa, Dolce Crème de Menthe *Heuchera*, *Nemesia fruticans* 'Blue Bird' and 'Safari White', summer snapdragon

EXPOSURE: Part shade/full sun in cool climates
WATER: Low to regular*
SOIL: Well-draining planting mix
FERTILIZER: Slow-release fertilizer in spring or liquid fertilizer every 14 days once plants are established
Regular water advisable only if using a fast-draining soil mix

BUILD IT! →

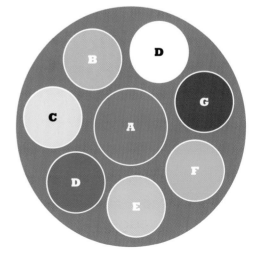

elegant exotica

Bromeliads and their kin bring a kaleidoscope of color and exceptional exotic shape to container gardens. They also produce some of the world's most dazzling flowers. Allow their glamorous looks to whisk you away to the ambience of a tropical clime.

PLANT LIST

A. *Neoregelia* 'Donger'

This clustering bromeliad features handsome rosettes of brightly colored green leaves blushed with rosy pink and edged in cream. Plants can grow 6 to 12 inches tall.

B. *Billbergia* 'Hallelujah'

Rich merlot and fuchsia urn-like foliage is animated with dramatic white and dark spotting. Plants produce spectacular rich reddish flower stalks topped with tubular, electric violet-blue flowers.

C. *Tillandsia cyanea* 'Emily'

Small shrub-like bromeliad with narrow green leaves forming a fine-textured rosette. Produces vibrant spear-shaped flower heads from which fragrant ultraviolet flowers emerge. Wet or mist foliage regularly, as plants do not have a foliage cup or "tank" to hold water.

HOW TO GROW IT

EXPOSURE: Part sun/bright shade
WATER: Mist the foliage or add distilled water to the cup or "tank" at the center of their foliage rosette; do not fill all the way as this can lead to rot. If water remains in the cup after 10 days, extract it with a kitchen baster before refilling.
SOIL: Light, fast-draining soil mix or cactus mix blended with one part peat moss or coconut coir. Bromeliads can rot if planted too deeply. If needed, position stakes or chopsticks around your plant to provide support until its roots grow and anchor it.
FERTILIZER: Epiphytes Delight (see Paxton Gale and Rainforest Flora, "Resource Guide," page 184) or 50% diluted all-purpose fertilizer low in copper every 14 days; feeding mature plants (3 years old and up) with a pinch of Epsom salts mixed with water can encourage blooming.

ABOVE LEFT: *Tillandsia cyanea* 'Emily'

ABOVE RIGHT: Adding peat moss makes for a lighter soil mix.

LEFT: *Billbergia* 'Hallelujah'

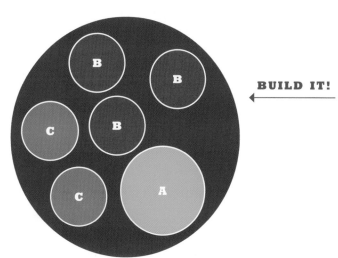

BUILD IT!

minty fresh

Crisp white and clean green light up the senses with wispy foliage, graphic shapes, and a scent of mint. The bold shapes of the containers topped with layers of texture bring freshness to a formal look.

PLANT LIST

A. Variegated Mint Bush

(*Prostanthera ovalifolia* 'Variegata') An upright, evergreen shrub with small, variegated mint-scented foliage. Grows 6 to 7 feet tall and produces profuse purple flowers in spring. Form of plant presents a soft texture and delicate glow that illuminates dim spaces.

B. *Lomandra longifolia* 'Breeze'

This clumping grasslike perennial grows 2 to 3 feet tall and wide. Its rich, green, fountain-like form provides sophisticated movement to a container. In spring, it produces slender yellow flower heads with a slight honey scent.

C. *Aeonium undulatum*

Bold green rosettes of spoon-shaped leaves distinguish this succulent. Rosettes can grow 1 to 2 feet wide on stalks 2 to 3 feet tall, providing a wonderful graphic element to containers.

D. *Dianella tasmanica* 'Variegata'

This 1- to 2-foot-tall strap-leaf plant has gray-green leaves boldly striped in white. In spring, it produces stalks with small, pale violet flowers followed by dark metallic-blue berries.

E. Spotted Dead Nettle

(*Lamium maculatum* 'Ghost') Tender-stemmed perennial grows 8 inches tall with a spread reaching up to 3 feet. Mint-green leaves are frosted with white and provide a charming filler for containers. Dainty pinkish purple flowers are produced from late spring through autumn.

Spotted dead nettle

HOW TO GROW IT

EXPOSURE: Part sun/part shade
WATER: Regular
SOIL: Well-draining planting mix
FERTILIZER: Slow-release fertilizer in spring or light feeding of liquid fertilizer once a month when plants are established

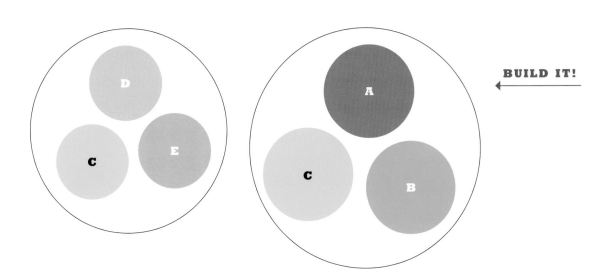

BUILD IT! ←

shimmering stripes

A trio of playfully striped containers set the stage for the electric contrast of shimmering silver and dark dramatic color. The informal look creates a style that is deliciously compelling.

A. Blackbird Spurge

(*Euphorbia* 'Blackbird') An attractive herbaceous perennial with deep dark foliage; color intensifies in full sun. It produces contrasting lime green flower bracts on red stems and looks exceptional in a container. Grows 1 to 3 feet tall with equal width. Note: When cut, euphorbias produce a white sticky sap that can irritate skin.

B. Bush Morning Glory

(*Convolvulus cneorum* 'Snow Angel') Sprawling shrub with satiny smooth, silver-gray leaves that produces pink-tinted flower buds that open white with yellow centers. Great plant for spilling over the edge of a container. Grows 2 to 4 feet tall and wide.

C. *Dichondra argentea* 'Silver Falls'

Vigorously trailing plant with spectacular silky silver foliage. Great spiller for a container. Grows 2 to 4 inches tall.

D. Black Scallop Carpet Bugle

(*Ajuga reptans* 'Black Scallop') Low, mat-forming groundcover has glossy purple-black leaves with a dimpled texture. Plant grows 4 to 6 inches tall and produces spikes of deep blue flowers from spring through summer.

E. Billy Buttons

(*Craspedia globosa*) This Australian daisy produces grasslike foliage that looks like liquid silver. It sends up a 2-foot flower stalk topped by a globe of tiny yellow flowers. Makes a great cut flower and foliar accent. Plants like full sun but tolerate part shade.

F. *Ozothamnus* 'County Park Silver'

Looking like a silver shag rug, this mat-forming perennial has a soft, fine-textured foliage that grows up to 3 inches tall with a potential spread of 2 feet.

TOP: Bush morning glory

BOTTOM: Blackbird spurge

HOW TO GROW IT

EXPOSURE: Full sun/part shade
WATER: Regular
SOIL: Well-draining planting mix
FERTILIZER: Slow-release fertilizer in spring or light feeding of liquid fertilizer every 14 days once plants are established

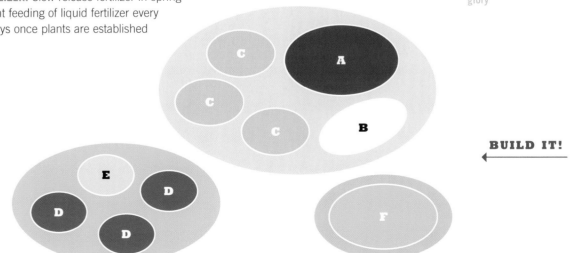

BUILD IT! ←

mod meadow

A lush planting is paired with a tall, sleek container to create the modern meadow. Rich rosy purple blossoms float above the perfect platform of cappuccino and dark chocolate foliage for a contained contemporary look.

A. New Zealand Sedge

(*Carex tenuiculmis* 'Cappuccino') This graceful, arching sedge features rich cappuccino color that shimmers in light. A beautiful accent, it forms a mound 12 to 16 inches tall and 24 inches wide.

B. Purple Coneflower

(*Echinacea purpurea* 'Bravado') The perennial North American native produces large rosy purple daisy flowers with smoldering orange centers from summer through autumn. It grows up to 2 feet tall, attracts butterflies and bees, and makes a great cut flower. Mix with grasses for that wild meadow look.

C. Sweet Potato Vine

(*Ipomoea batatas* 'Blackie') This vigorous ornamental vine has deeply lobed chocolate-purple foliage, which lends a very dramatic look. Plants grow 6 to 10 inches tall and up to 6 feet long. Plants can be cut back to control growth.

HOW TO GROW IT

EXPOSURE: Full sun
WATER: Regular
SOIL: Well-draining planting mix
FERTILIZER: Slow-release fertilizer in spring or liquid fertilizer every 14 days once plants are established

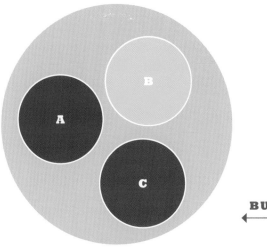

BUILD IT! ←

TOP: Purple coneflower   **BOTTOM:** Sweet potato vine

wine punch

Neon-like highlights and warm wine tones
are tempered by soothingly cool blue-green
detailed with deep burgundy. The glossy
deep olive container is the perfect contrast
to set off this blaze of color.

A. New Zealand Flax

(*Phormium* '*Sundowner*') The smoldering, strappy leaves of this flax lily are further emphasized by strikingly striped margins of rose and pink. For containers, start with a 1-gallon size as this plant can grow up to 8 feet tall.

B. Painted Lady Echeveria

(*Echeveria nodulosa*) This succulent produces icy blue-green rosettes of foliage painted with filigree-like markings of rich red. Plants grow up to 5 inches in diameter and can branch up to 1½ feet tall. Group them in the container for bold effect.

C. *Heucherella* 'Sweet Tea'

This plant is primarily grown for its foliage. Its soft mounding form is set ablaze with its stunning foliage color of rich, coppery orange and burgundy. It stays relatively low at 20 inches and gives a softening effect when placed where it can grow over the lip of a container.

ABOVE LEFT: New Zealand flax

ABOVE RIGHT: *Heucherella* 'Sweet Tea'

LEFT: Painted lady echeveria

HOW TO GROW IT

EXPOSURE: Part sun/full sun in cool climates
WATER: Regular
SOIL: Fast-draining soil mix or cactus mix
FERTILIZER: Slow-release fertilizer in spring or light feeding of liquid fertilizer once a month when plants are established

BUILD IT! →

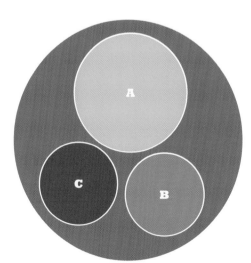

beachside style

This grouping of containers brings together sculptural plants that celebrate the look of the sea and love to soak up the sun.

A. Paddle Plant

(Kalanchoe luciae) This structural succulent looks like a cluster of colorful clamshells. Large paddle-like leaves blushed in ruby red. At the height of summer, these plants produce silvery stalks with clusters of tiny flowers. Protect from frost.

B. Red-Hot Poker

(Kniphofia uvaria) This perennial plant forms clumps of fine-textured grasslike leaves. In late spring and summer, they send up spikes of brilliant orange-yellow tubular flowers that hummingbirds love. Plants can grow 2 to 3 feet tall.

C. *Agave desmettiana* 'Variegata'

This small, statured agave produces a well-composed rosette of curved green leaves illuminated by smooth, vibrant yellow edges. They are reminiscent of a sea anemone resting on a coral reef.

D. Red Pencil Tree

(Euphorbia tirucalli **'Sticks on Fire')** This succulent shrub looks something like branching undersea coral. Its succulent stems take on tones from red to gold and look as though they're swaying in an ocean current. It should be handled with care, as it produces a milky sap when damaged that can burn skin.

HOW TO GROW IT

EXPOSURE: Full sun/part shade
WATER: Low to regular for kalanchoe and kniphofia; low for agave and euphorbia
SOIL: Cactus mix or fast-draining planting mix
FERTILIZER: 50% diluted or low-concentration all-purpose liquid fertilizer applied once in spring and again in fall

BUILD IT!

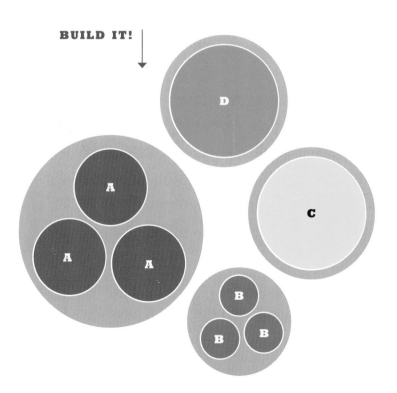

TOP: Red-hot poker   **BOTTOM:** Red pencil tree

spring forward

Capture the sensation of spring by complementing a clean, green container with a cheerful combination of color. Start with the newness of crisp white, youthful yellow, blushing blue, and fresh gorgeous greens.

A. Feverfew

(Chrysanthemum parthenium) An attractive perennial with refreshing chartreuse foliage and feathery form. Produces button-like white daisies with rich yellow centers and grows 1 to 3 feet tall.

B. Persian Buttercup

(Ranunculus asiaticus) Fernlike leaves form rounded clumps and bear large and often densely layered colorful flowers. Plants grow 8 to 10 inches tall and bloom in spring.

C. Primrose

(Primula obconica) Evergreen perennial forms soft, rounded rosettes of medium green leaves from which flower stalks emerge in late winter and spring. Stalks are topped with large broad clusters of 1½- to 2-inch-wide blooms in white, pink, salmon, lavender, or purple. This plant grows up to a foot tall and wide. For this composition, use white-blooming varieties.

D. Bacopa

(Sutera cordata) Cascading stemmed creeper has sweet, heart-shaped green leaves and produces continuous blooms of small, five-petal, golden-throated flowers. Flower colors come in white, pink, or lavender. Great plant for creating a cascading effect.

E. Blue Star Creeper

(Pratia pedunculata) Fluffy textured groundcover with tiny leaves explodes with small, star-shaped blue flowers in late spring and summer. Makes an excellent filler plant.

F. Johnny-Jump-Up

(Viola tricolor) Plucky wild pansies reach 6 to 12 inches tall and produce perky flower faces in a variety of cheerful colors.

G. Licorice Plant

(Helichrysum petiolare) Mounding groundcover or shrub with downy textured arching stems and soft, woolly rounded leaves. Comes in soft gray and luminous light chartreuse.

Clockwise from top: Feverfew, licorice plant, blue star creeper, bacopa

HOW TO GROW IT

EXPOSURE: Part sun/full sun in cool climates
WATER: Regular
SOIL: Well-draining planting mix
FERTILIZER: Slow-release fertilizer in spring or all-purpose liquid fertilizer applied every 14 days once plants are established

BUILD IT! →

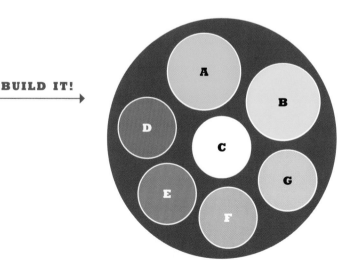

gold rush

A bonanza of bold foliage amps up the style factor of these glossy golden containers. Spikes sprout, foliage fills, and color thrills, creating a feast for the eyes.

A. *Phormium* 'Alison Blackman'

Clump-forming perennial with variegated olive, orange, and yellow swordlike leaves. Provides excellent structure and a vertical accent to a container. Grows 3 to 4 feet tall.

B. *Heuchera* 'Melting Fire'

Clump-forming perennial with vibrant deep maroon ruffled foliage. Provides a rich burst of color as well as texture. In spring and summer, plants send up airy sprays of tiny white flowers. Plant grows 8 to 12 inches tall and 12 inches wide.

C. *Hebe ochracea* 'James Stirling'

Compact evergreen shrub with arching, twisted stems covered in juniper-like ochre-yellow leaves. Very striking accent for a container. Grows up to 1½ feet tall and 2 feet wide in part sun.

D. *Hemizygia* 'Candy Kisses'

Upright perennial plant with wine purple stems covered with striking cream-and-green variegated leaves. Great plant for brightening up a container. Produces spikes of pinkish plum flowers. Plants can grow up to 3 feet tall and 2½ feet wide.

E. *Plectranthus* hybrid 'Troy's Gold'

This sprawling herbaceous perennial has textured gold foliage splashed with green. It grows 6 to 12 inches tall and up to 3 feet wide. Contrasts beautifully with darker-colored plants. Makes for a great rambling or spilling element in containers.

F. *Deschampsia cespitosa* 'Northern Lights'

Small, upright clumping grass with narrow variegated green-and-cream leaf blades blushed with rosy pink. Tufted form adds fine texture and softness to a container. Plants grow a foot tall and wide.

TOP: *Hemizygia* 'Candy Kisses' **BOTTOM:** *Plectranthus* 'Troy's Gold' spills over the pot's rim

HOW TO GROW IT

EXPOSURE: Full sun/part shade
WATER: Regular
SOIL: Well-draining planting mix
FERTILIZER: Slow-release fertilizer in spring or a light feeding of liquid fertilizer every 14 days once plants are established

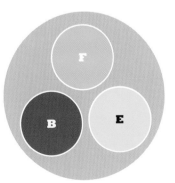

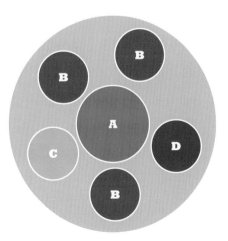

BUILD IT!

electric lemonade

Bold color, texture, and form add up to a sizzling tropical arrangement that steals the spotlight.

A. Canna 'Pretoria'

Packs a punch with bold luscious leaves in tropical tones of vibrant yellow and splendid grass green. This 4- to 6-foot-tall perennial tops itself off with tantalizing tangerine blossoms summer through fall.

B. New Zealand Flax

(Phormium 'Yellow Wave')
Versatile evergreen strap-leaf plant with bright yellow leaves edged in rich green margins. Its frolicking foliage is a great way to add a splash of color and movement to any composition.

C. Honey Bush

(Melianthus major)
This bold-looking perennial shrub has bluish green tropical foliage with dramatic sawtooth edges. The sprawling plant can grow 6 to 12 feet tall, but can be pruned back and kept much smaller in a container. In late winter and early spring, it produces architectural spikes of red flowers. Makes a great accent plant.

D. Sweet Potato Vine

(Ipomoea batatas 'Margarita')
Vigorously growing vine with stunning bright lime green foliage. Looks amazing when positioned to spill over the side of a container. Plants grow 6 to 10 inches tall and can cascade up to 6 feet. Plants can be cut back to control their growth.

ABOVE LEFT: Sweet potato vine

ABOVE RIGHT: Canna 'Pretoria'

HOW TO GROW IT

EXPOSURE: Full sun/part shade
WATER: Regular
SOIL: Well-draining planting mix
FERTILIZER: Slow-release fertilizer in spring or all-purpose liquid fertilizer applied every 14 days once plants are established

BUILD IT! →

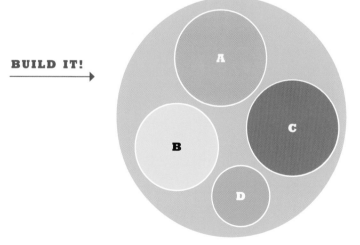

This Japanese-inspired combination creates
a modern contrast. A rigid vertical form shoots
upward from a soft mound of vibrant color,
carefully balanced with a rounded organic
container.

A. Variegated Striped Rush

(*Baumea rubiginosa* **'Variegata'**) An upright, grasslike rush with slender, flat leaves animated by golden stripes of color. Grows up to 1½ feet tall.

B. Scotch Moss

(*Sagina subulata* **'Aurea'**) A lime green to yellow mossy perennial used as a dense, mounding groundcover. Great plant for filling gaps in container gardens.

HOW TO GROW IT

EXPOSURE: Full sun/part shade
WATER: Regular
SOIL: Well-draining planting mix
FERTILIZER: Slow-release fertilizer in spring or all-purpose liquid fertilizer every 14 days once plants are established

Left to right: Scotch moss, variegated striped rush

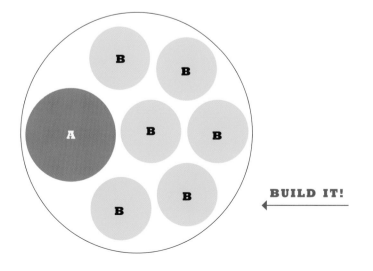

BUILD IT! ←

touch
of bronze

Rich reddish purples,
shimmering golds, and
glossy greens bring
welcome softness to the
stonelike surface of this
rustic container.

A. Lily-of-the-Valley Shrub

(*Pieris* 'Forest Flame') Robust red spring growth fades to pink before giving way to mature glossy, dark-green foliage. This shrub produces profuse clusters of unique urn-shaped white flowers and can reach 10 feet tall.

B. Autumn Fern

(*Dryopteris erythrosora*) The firm and feathery new growth of this hardy wood fern is a medley of copper, pink, and gold tones that turn rust-colored in autumn. It grows up to 2 feet and offers an inviting textural accent.

C. Azalea 'Little John'

Reddish purple leaves provide a dramatic palette to this rounded shrub that can grow up to 6 feet tall. Excellent as a focal point or contrasting filler plant.

HOW TO GROW IT

EXPOSURE: Part shade
WATER: Regular
SOIL: Acid-loving planting mix or well-draining planting mix
FERTILIZER: Slow-release fertilizer in spring or a light feeding of liquid fertilizer applied once in spring, summer, and fall

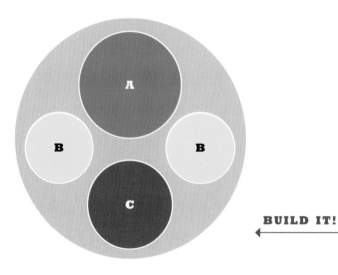

BUILD IT! ←

TOP: Autumn fern   **BOTTOM:** Azalea 'Little John'

burnished splendor

A vivid fusion of foliage texture and color highlights the glazed sheen of these contemporary containers. Burnished tones of burgundy and bronze are tempered by vibrant greens to create a smoldering display.

A. Evening Glow Mirror Plant

(*Coprosma* 'Evening Glow') This New Zealand shrub has upright form and glossy green leaves splashed with gold. Evergreen foliage takes on orange and red color in cooler temperatures. Makes a beautiful addition to a container. Can grow up to 5 feet tall and 3 to 4 feet wide.

B. Golden Sweet Flag

(*Acorus gramineus* 'Ogon') Evergreen grasslike foliage is green striped with bright yellow. Foliage is pleasantly aromatic when crushed. Neat 10-inch blades provide both an arching and a vertical accent.

C. Scotch Moss

(*Sagina subulata* 'Aurea') Lime green to yellow mossy perennial forms a dense mounding groundcover that is great for filling gaps between plantings. Makes for a vibrant accent in containers.

D. Bronze New Zealand Flax

(*Phormium*) Upright strappy leaves of bronze with hints of burgundy bring evergreen vertical drama. Makes for a striking focal element or engaging accent in containers. Start with smaller 1-gallon sizes, as this plant can reach 6 to 8 feet tall.

E. 'Gulf Stream' Heavenly Bamboo

(*Nandina domestica* 'Gulf Stream') Bamboo-like shrub is covered with fine-textured foliage that is soothing blue-green in summer, turning to a rich red in winter. Grows 3 to 3½ feet tall and 1½ feet wide. Makes for a good filler in containers. Prune occasionally to encourage dense, lush foliage.

F. Pheasant's-Tail Grass

(*Anemanthele lessoniana*) Billowy, clump-forming grass with a gorgeous, graceful form. Olive blades become tinged in orange and amber color with age. Produces feathery flower heads in summer that shimmer in light. Can grow 3 feet tall and wide.

G. *Heuchera* 'Purple Petticoats'

Clump-forming plant has mounds of dark purple frilly foliage with bright purple undersides. Produces delicate sprays of cream-colored flowers in late spring. Creates a rich accent in a container. Grows 1 to 1½ feet tall and 1½ feet to 2 feet wide.

H. *Cordyline australis* 'Dark Star'

Palmlike plants with woody trunks produce fountains of straplike reddish bronze leaves. Plants provide a tropical look and serve as a great focal point or accent in containers. Can grow up to 20 feet tall and 8 feet wide.

Golden sweet flag

BUILD IT!

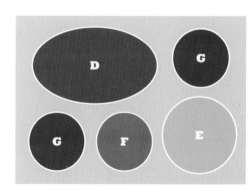

EXPOSURE: Full sun/part shade
WATER: Regular
SOIL: Well-draining planting mix
FERTILIZER: Slow-release fertilizer in spring or a light feeding of liquid fertilizer monthly once plants are established

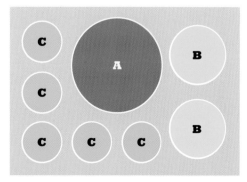

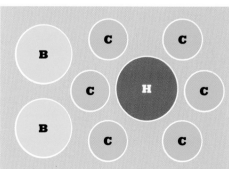

captivating carnivores

With their otherworldly form and fantastical flowers, carnivorous plants add a certain allure to any container garden. These fascinating plants catch and consume insects to satisfy their nutritional needs. Use them in a glazed or ceramic container for a striking look.

A. Pitcher Plant

(Sarracenia) Rosettes of structural chartreuse "pitchers" are flushed with ruby reds, deep oranges, or snowy whites. Streaks of colorful pigment on the foliage add to the allure. Plants grow 10 to 24 inches tall and produce flowers on single stalks that will stop you in your tracks with their ethereal form.

B. *Sarracenia purpurea*

The funnel-shaped "pitchers" on this plant vary from green to purple, and flowers are burgundy, green, or pink. Plants grow 6 to 12 inches tall.

C. Venus Flytrap

(Dionaea muscipula) This tender perennial forms a rosette of leaves topped with an open clamshell-like structure that closes like a trap when triggered by touch. These "traps" can be bright green, rich red, or a combination of the two; if they turn black, which happens as they age, just pinch them off. Plants grow 6 inches tall and wide.

D. Cape Sundew

(Drosera capensis) Red filament structures lining the leaves produce a dewdrop essence that gives the plant a mysterious glow and airy appearance. These plants grow 6 inches tall and wide. In spring, they produce five-petal flowers in pinkish purple.

HOW TO GROW IT

EXPOSURE: Full sun
WATER: Damp/wet
SOIL: Low-nutrient soil mix (containing a 1:1 ratio of peat moss or coconut coir and pumice
FERTILIZER: None recommended. If fertilizing is needed, mist plants with a 50% dilution of Epiphytes Delight fertilizer (see Paxton Gate and Rainforest Flora, "Resource Guide," page 184)

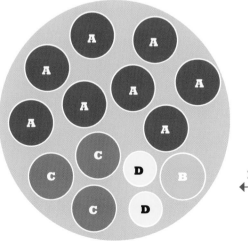

BUILD IT!

TOP: Pitcher plant   **BOTTOM:** Venus flytrap

111

cherry firefall

An arching form explodes out of a subtly textured black synthetic container. Cherry foliage skyrockets like fireworks in flight, while a soft, cool blue-gray blanket of color overflows and balances the intensity.

A. *Cordyline* 'Festival Grass'

Vibrant cherry-red strap-leaf foliage frolics like a fireworks display from this small cordyline. Grows into a 3-foot-tall and -wide fountainlike clump that annually produces stalks topped with a spray of tiny, starry white flowers. Makes a beautiful container accent or specimen.

B. *Adenanthos cuneatus* 'Coral Drift'

A beautiful low-growing Australian shrub with shell-shaped leaves. New growth is flushed in pinkish red. Plants produce small, tubular ruby red flowers in spring. Grows 2 to 4 feet tall and 3 to 5 feet wide.

C. Gray Honey Myrtle

(*Melaleuca incana* 'Prostrate Form')

A low-growing woolly gray shrub with a cascading form. Small, woolly, needle-like leaves provide a soft texture. Plants produce small cream-white bottlebrush flowers in late spring through summer. Plants can grow 1 to 2 feet tall and 4 to 6 feet wide.

Adenanthos cuneatus 'Coral Drift' with *Cordyline* 'Festival Grass' in the background

HOW TO GROW IT

EXPOSURE: Full sun
WATER: Low
SOIL: Well-draining planting mix or cactus mix
FERTILIZER: Slow-release, low-phosphorus fertilizer applied annually (*Adenanthos cuneatus* 'Coral Drift' is sensitive to fertilizers high in phosphorus)

BUILD IT!

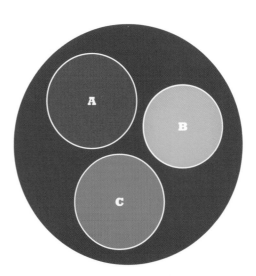

greens and beans

Greens and climbing beans are the perfect edibles to grow in a container because they are easy to maintain and harvest. Combine them with billowy bronze fennel to create a container garden that looks surprisingly sophisticated and tastes good too!

A. Bronze Fennel

Upright perennial herb with airy bronze foliage that resembles plumes of smoke. Delicious anise-flavored leaves and seeds for salads, fish, meats, and breads. Grows up to 4 feet tall.

B. Bok Choy (green and violet varieties)

Asian greens that form loose heads of tender, crisp, and mildly flavored savory leaves that are perfect sautéed or stir-fried.

C. Scarlet Runner Beans

Gorgeous green twining vines pair with bright green leaves that produce clusters of vivid scarlet flowers. Flat, dark green bean pods are edible and tasty when young. Vines will need support.

D. Looseleaf Lettuce (green and red varieties)

Looseleaf lettuce forms rosettes of fast-growing, tender, and delicious lettuce greens. These easy-to-pick greens are perfect for adding color and subtle taste to salads.

HOW TO GROW IT

EXPOSURE: Full sun
WATER: Keep soil evenly moist
SOIL: Well-draining planting mix
FERTILIZER: Dig in additional organic compost before planting or apply one application of slow-release fertilizer at planting; if using liquid fertilizer, feed every 14 days during growing season

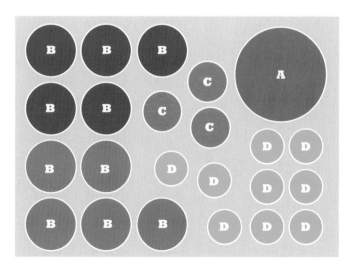

← **BUILD IT!**

TOP: Scarlet runner bean **BOTTOM:** Romaine 'Remus'

Create a single planter with edibles that can provide ingredients for several combinations of delicious dishes.

A. 'Early Girl' Tomato

This early producing, tall-growing tomato is a garden favorite. It dependably produces tasty 4- to 5-ounce tomatoes. Great for short-season gardens.

B. Purple Ruffles Basil

Not only is this basil tasty, but its dark ruffled foliage looks beautiful too. It provides a striking visual accent by adding rich color to a container. Plants grow from 12 to 18 inches tall.

C. Garlic Chives

An easy-to-grow perennial whose flat, tender leaves taste like a cross between garlic and onion. Great for topping soups, salads, and pasta. Plants grow 18 to 24 inches tall.

D. Jalapeño Chile

Spice up your meals and your landscape. Bushy green plants grow 18 to 24 inches tall and produce thick-walled peppers resembling emerald green ornaments.

HOW TO GROW IT

EXPOSURE: Full sun
WATER: Keep soil evenly moist
SOIL: Well-draining planting mix
FERTILIZER: Dig in additional organic compost before planting or apply one application of slow-release fertilizer at planting; if using liquid fertilizer, feed every 14 days during growing season.

TOP: 'Early Girl' tomato   **BOTTOM:** Jalapeño chile

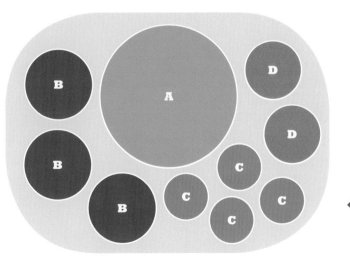

BUILD IT! ←

117

citrus and chocolate

A chocolate-brown container comes to life with
a colorful combination of lemon-lime and golden
shades of greens.

A. *Salvia elegans* 'Golden Delicious'

This perennial, which grows 12 to 24 inches tall, produces bright yellow foliage with a delicious pineapple scent. In late summer, bright nectar-filled red flowers appear, attracting hummingbirds and butterflies.

B. Lemon Twist *Solenostemon* (Coleus)

Upright annual 12 to 24 inches tall with lacy, lemony leaves edged with crimson. Use this plant's foliage for brilliant textural interest.

C. Japanese Sweet Flag

(*Acorus gramineus* 'Ogon') Grasslike tufts of narrow, arching golden yellow leaf blades tinged with green reach up to 10 inches long. Use as a filler for a wispy, willowy look.

D. *Heuchera* Dolce Key Lime Pie

Mounded perennial plant of scalloped, heart-shaped, bright lime green leaves grows up to 16 inches tall. Makes a stunning accent plant.

E. Supertunia White Petunia

This 6- to 10-inch-long trailing plant is covered with snow-white blossoms all season long.

F. Creeping Jenny

(*Lysimachia nummularia* 'Goldilocks') Glossy, heart-shaped chartreuse leaves cover the stems of this low-growing trailer, bringing a jolt of vibrant color to any composition.

G. Superbells Yellow Chiffon *Calibrachoa*

This petunia-like plant produces a prolific amount of lemon yellow flowers from early spring to the light frosts of late autumn. Grows 7 to 10 inches tall and makes a wonderful cascading plant.

H. Bacopa

(*Sutera cordata* 'Snowstorm Giant Snowflake') Petite white flowers cover this cascading creeper. A prolific bloomer, it produces flowers all season against a backdrop of sweet, heart-shaped green foliage.

I. *Euphorbia* 'Diamond Frost'

This lacy plant grows 12 to 18 inches tall and continuously produces an abundance of cloud-like dainty white blossoms. Its mounded habit makes it an excellent filler plant.

Clockwise from upper right: Creeping Jenny, bacopa, Superbells Yellow Chiffon *Calibrachoa*, *Salvia elegans* 'Golden Delicious', Japanese sweet flag, Dolce Key Lime Pie *Heuchera*, Supertunia White petunia, 'Diamond Frost' *Euphorbia*, Lemon Twist *Solenostemon*

EXPOSURE: Part shade/full sun in cool climates
WATER: Regular
SOIL: Well-draining planting mix
FERTILIZER: Slow-release fertilizer in spring or liquid fertilizer every 14 days once plants are established

BUILD IT! →

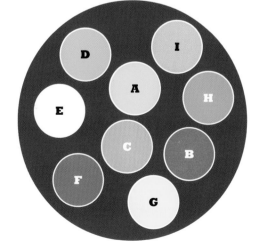

suspended
style

The unique form
of this spilling plant
paired with a con-
temporary container
creates a dramatic
focal point on high.

A. *Hoya carnosa* 'Krinkle Kurl'

Trailing plant with contorted succulent leaves that cascade on ropelike stems. Stems can grow up to 20 feet long to create a stunning textural look spilling from tall or elevated containers. Produces fragrant clusters of waxy pinkish red flowers.

HOW TO GROW IT

EXPOSURE: Part sun/bright shade
WATER: Regular; water sparingly in winter
SOIL: Well-draining planting mix or cactus mix
FERTILIZER: 50% diluted all-purpose fertilizer every 2 months during spring and summer
Note: For Hoya carnosa *'Krinkle Kurl' only*

TOP LEFT: Parrot's beak

BOTTOM LEFT: *Dichondra argentea* 'Silver Falls'

TOP RIGHT: *Sedum sieboldii*

BOTTOM RIGHT: *Sedum morganianum* 'Donkey Tail'

Other Textural Hanging Plants

» *Dichondra argentea* 'Silver Falls'

» Parrot's beak (*Lotus maculatus* 'Gold Flash' or *Lotus berthelotii*)

» *Rhipsalis*

» *Scaevola*

» *Sedum morganianum* 'Donkey Tail'

» *Sedum sieboldii*

» Strawberry geranium (*Saxifraga stolonifera*)

» String of pearls (*Senecio rowleyanus*)

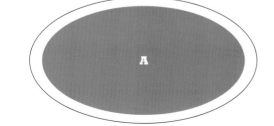

 BUILD IT!

succulent chic

Sky blue containers team up with jewel-like succulents and the glamour of tumbled glass to produce this ultra-vivid scene.

A. *Aeonium arboreum* 'Zwartkop'

Striking pinwheels of near black foliage grow on top of textured brown stems. Plants can branch or remain single-stemmed growing 3 to 4 feet tall. Very dramatic plant for a container.

B. Fan Aloe

(Aloe plicatilis) A sculpturally stunning succulent featuring fanlike heads of blue-green round-tipped foliage. Plants are slow growing but can reach 4 to 6 feet tall and wide over time. As plants mature, they produce stalks of tubular scarlet-orange blossoms in late winter and early spring.

C. *Echeveria* 'Black Knight'

Small, compact succulent rosettes of narrow-tipped chocolate-black foliage provide a very dramatic look. In autumn, plants produce stalks topped with brilliant red urn-shaped flowers.

D. *Echeveria* 'Perle von Nürnberg'

Medium, compact succulent rosettes of pinkish blue rounded leaves. Plant color looks as if it is glowing.

E. *Kalanchoe pumila*

Low-growing, spreading succulent plant with rosy gray rounded leaves covered in soft white hairs that lend a frosty sheen. Plants can grow 8 to 12 inches tall and produce clusters of pinkish purple flowers in spring. Great plant for spilling over the sides of a container.

F. Cape Blanco Stonecrop

(Sedum spathulifolium 'Cape Blanco'*)* Small spoon-shaped leaves are packed into rosettes on trailing stems. Foliage is bluish green tinged with reddish purple. A great textural filler.

G. *Agave parryi* var. *truncata*

Handsome greenish gray 2- to 3-foot-wide compact rosettes studded with attractive deep brownish purple spines. Provides bold structural interest.

H. Blue Chalk Sticks

(Senecio serpens) Small, fingerlike ground cover with luminous powdery blue-green succulent leaves. Great plant for filling space and creating vibrant texture in a container.

Echeveria 'Black Knight' in the foreground and *Echeveria* 'Perle von Nürnberg' in the background

EXPOSURE: Full sun/part shade
WATER: Low
SOIL: Cactus mix or fast-draining soil mix*
FERTILIZER: 50% diluted or low-concentration all-purpose fertilizer applied once in spring and again in fall

BUILD IT!

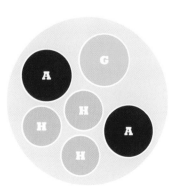

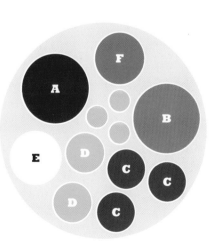

black cherry sundae

The textural glaze of the container sets the tone for the plant palette, which echoes its luscious, dripping colors.

A. *Cordyline* Renegade 'Tana'

This beautiful clump-forming cordyline puts on a striking show with rich purple, nearly black arching strap-leaf foliage. Its form and dramatic evergreen foliage make it the perfect container centerpiece. It grows 2 to 3 feet tall and wide.

B. Blue Fescue

(***Festuca glauca*** 'Elijah Blue')
Clumping grass with vibrant silver-blue foliage grows 8 inches tall and provides a rich contrast to dark colors. The perfect filler plant.

C. *Hebe pimeleoides* 'Quicksilver'

A small arching shrub composed of striking black stems contrasted by small gray leaves. Offers an interesting look when allowed to grow through other foliage. Plant grows 8 to 12 inches tall and wide.

D. *Sedum* x 'Vera Jameson'

Spreading plant with succulent purple-gray leaves and ruby red star-shaped flowers. Grows 8 to 12 inches tall and 1½ feet wide. Place near the lip of your container for a cascading effect.

Hebe pimeleoides 'Quicksilver' with *Cordyline* Renegade 'Tana' in the background

HOW TO GROW IT

EXPOSURE: Full sun/part shade
WATER: Regular
SOIL: Well-draining planting mix or cactus mix
FERTILIZER: Slow-release fertilizer in spring or a light feeding of liquid fertilizer monthly once plants are established

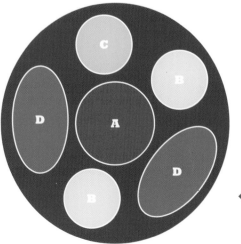

BUILD IT!

wild
and woolly

Vertical container gardens have become a recent fascination. Try using Woolly Pockets, or look for other vertical garden systems at retailers or online. Not only do they make for engaging space-saving container gardens, but they can also become works of art.

A. *Aeonium*

Succulents with foliage arranged in a whimsical pinwheel formation. Full sun where cool and part sun in other locations. Regular water.

B. Bromeliads (assorted varieties)

Tropical color and foliage arranged in arching rosettes. Periodically fill center of foliage cup three-quarters full with water.

C. Firecracker Plant

(*Russelia equisetiformis*) Trailing, almost leafless stems produce a profusion of red tubular flowers. Great as a cascading plant. Sun/part sun and regular water.

D. Foxtail Asparagus Fern

(*Asparagus densiflorus* 'Myers') Soft, sculptural foliage. Full sun where cool. Part shade in other locations and regular water.

E. *Pelargonium* x *hortorum* 'Mrs. Pollock'

Striking plant of vibrant color. Rich reds flare and yellows shimmer on leaves.

F. *Peperomia ferreyrae*

Structural succulent with thick stems and trough-shaped leaves. Part sun and shade. Let dry between waterings.

G. String of Bananas or Fishhooks

(*Senecio radicans*) Cascading succulent with striking foliage that resembles little bananas or fishhooks. Part sun. Regular water.

HOW TO BUILD USING WOOLLY POCKETS

Hang Woolly Pocket by its grommets, then fill it two-thirds full with rich, fast-draining soil.

Add plants. Start with 4-inch and 6-inch sizes. If there is room, try using 1-gallon plants.

Exposure and watering depend on plants used. Consult manufacturer instructions (woollypockets.com).

TOP: *Peperomia ferreyrae* and *Aeonium*

BOTTOM: *Pelargonium* x *hortorum* 'Mrs. Pollock' in the foreground and firecracker plant in the background

BUILD IT!

Pocket on facing page, middle row, far right

Culture and Care

Container gardens need a bit more tending than plants in the ground. They dry out faster, have less soil to draw nutrients from, and are more vulnerable to extreme temperatures. But—as you'll learn in this section—with the right tools and a little know-how, it's easy to keep them looking their best and thriving. And if problems do arise, this section will also tell you how to remedy them.

With the right care, your container garden will be productive for seasons to come.

your tools

A trusty set of hand tools is a must-have for container gardening projects. Look for tools made of high-quality steel—anything described as tempered, heat tempered, or forged is your best bet. Comfort is important, too, so hold the tool in your hand and see how it feels before you buy it. Ergonomically designed tools that provide a user-friendly grip and reduce wrist stress are a smart choice and are widely available.

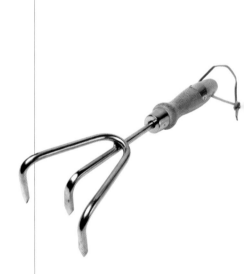

HAND TROWEL A necessity for every gardener, this hard-working implement is for digging, as well as planting and lifting plants. It's also helpful for transferring soil to containers and adding mulches or top dressings.

TRANSPLANTING TROWEL The narrow spade of this type of trowel is perfect for potting small plants and digging in tight spaces.

SCOOP Roomier than a trowel, a scoop is handy for transferring soil to a container or adding top dressings.

HAND FORK WITH TINES Great for loosening and scoring the surface of soil in preparation for planting, as well as raking and weeding compact spots.

GARDEN SHEARS For removing spent flowers, cutting back foliage, and shaping growth.

LONG TWEEZERS Designed for meticulous cleanup, arranging, and grooming.

WATERING CAN Handy for easy, portable watering. If you prefer, look for ones made of light plastic with a comfortable grip—they tend to be easier to tote around than their heavier metal counterparts.

HAND PRUNERS Used for pruning and cutting, there are two basic types: anvil and bypass. Anvil pruners (top) push a sharp blade against a flat surface (the anvil); bypass pruners have two curved blades that operate more like scissors. Anvil pruners are excellent for removing dead growth, but they're bulkier than bypass pruners and can bruise green growth. Bypass pruners (bottom) make cleaner cuts and don't require as much pressure to operate. They're better all-purpose pruners.

BRUSH Helpful for dusting and grooming.

WIDGER A cross between a trowel and a dibber (a tapered implement for poking holes in soil), widgers are excellent instruments for getting into cramped spaces or for transplanting smaller plants.

watering

P roper watering is essential for a healthy garden, especially a container garden. Because potted plants grow in a limited amount of soil, their access to moisture is also limited. In very hot, dry weather, plants may even need watering more than once a day.

ENOUGH BUT NOT TOO MUCH

How do you know when plants need a drink? Sure signs are wilting, drying leaves, or cracked, parched soil. But it's best not to wait until things get to that point. Check your plants periodically by poking a finger into the soil up to your middle knuckle. If the soil feels dry, it's probably time to water. You can also use a chopstick or a moisture meter instead of your finger. Keep in mind, though, that if your pot isn't draining properly, feeling the top inch of soil can be deceiving. (See "Check drainage," page 135.)

Overwatering can be just as harmful as not watering enough. In fact, it's one of the most common ways to kill a plant. If your plant is wilted and the soil is moist, the roots are probably drowning down below and your plant could be headed for a premature death. Soil that remains wet, sticky, and cool could also indicate that the plant is waterlogged. If that's the case, let the soil dry out before watering again.

When you do water, be thorough, saturating plants enough that water runs out the bottom of the container. If you have a dish under your container, be sure to empty it. Standing water can back up into the container and drown the roots, as well as create a breeding ground for mosquitoes and other pests.

For containers that lack drainage holes (see page 37 for how to add drainage holes), be careful to saturate only the top one-quarter of the soil. Then let that dry before watering again. You don't want to end up with standing water inside the container.

If you live in a region that experiences only a few freezes during the winter, thorough watering adds insulation that can help your plants survive without moving them indoors. Water in the late morning so that roots can take up water before temperatures drop, and don't wet the foliage.

Misting the foliage with water is a quick way of giving humidity-loving plants the moisture they need.

care tips

》 If a garden hose has been sitting out in the sun, be sure to let the water run until it's cool before turning it on your containers. Hot water can shock roots.

》 Succulents and plants with fuzzy, textured surfaces don't appreciate overhead watering. Moisture on their foliage can cause damage or invite fungus to develop. Try to water under the foliage.

》 If soil is not absorbing water, one trick is to poke holes in the soil with a chopstick and pour water over the holes.

WAYS TO WATER

There are several ways to get moisture to your plants. The one you choose should depend on the size and location of your containers as well as your daily routine. However you decide to water, always apply it in a gentle stream, drip, or spray. This prevents displacement of the soil and reduces potential damage to plants with delicate stems, flowers, and foliage.

Always water early in the day so that if foliage gets wet, sun and wind will help dry it off before nightfall, preventing disease. This schedule also deters slugs and snails, which like to frequent moist places at night.

Watering Can
Watering cans are a manageable, handheld way to water your containers. They are a great choice if you have a small garden or space. To apply water gently, use a *rose,* or shower attachment, that affixes to the spout. Depending on what they're made of, watering cans can be cumbersome to carry around. Consider one made of light plastic with a comfortable grip.

Garden Hose
A hose is a must for larger spaces. Attachments like spray guns, fan nozzles, and rain wands offer a gentle and effective way to water plants in containers.

Soaking
Soaking is an ideal method for hanging baskets and small containers. It's also good for terra-cotta containers, which absorb water through their sides (and lose water quickly through evaporation). A thorough soak early in the day is an efficient way to revive plants when the soil has become overly dry. Simply fill a clean tub or bucket one-third full of water, and submerge your container until the water comes just to the bottom of the rim. Allow the container to soak for 20 to 30 minutes, then set the plant in a shady location to recover.

Drip Irrigation
If your daily routine calls for a time-saving and efficient way to water, drip irrigation could be the perfect solution. It directs water where you want it with the touch of a button or turn of a knob. These systems can hook right up to a hose bib or water line. Not only do they reduce the time you spend hand-watering, they also save water by delivering it only where needed. Drip-irrigation systems do require some upkeep to function smoothly and efficiently.

One other aspect to consider is that drip-irrigation systems are not particularly attractive, but you can camouflage the tubing—and protect it from damage—by running it behind your containers. Supplies are available at some garden centers, larger hardware stores, irrigation supply stores, or even online (see "Resource Guide," page 184).

Water-Conserving Strategies
» Use unthirsty, drought-tolerant plants such as succulents, as well as plants from Mediterranean climates.

» Collect rainwater and use it to irrigate plants.

» Add mulch to the soil surface to reduce evaporation.

CHECK DRAINAGE

When water doesn't drain freely after watering, it may mean the container's drain hole is blocked. You can check by turning the pot on its side and probing with your finger to clear any blockage.

If the hole is clear and drainage is still a problem, try elevating your container on bricks, pot feet, or stones; or add extra holes to the bottom of the container (see page 37).

Conversely, if water drains too fast, your potting mix may be so dry that it has pulled away from the sides of your container. As a result, water simply rolls over the soil, down the inner sides of the container, and out of the drain hole without saturating the soil. To remedy this situation, try the soaking method to rehydrate the soil, or place a hose on slow drip in the container and let it run until the soil is saturated.

care tip

» Don't put outdoor containers in saucers unless they're needed to protect surfaces. Water that collects can become stagnant, bringing pests and inviting root rot. If you do have standing water, a kitchen baster is handy for removing the excess.

LEFT: A showerhead attachment gently distributes water to container plantings without damaging delicate foliage or flowers.

FACING PAGE, TOP: Plants in containers can dry out faster than they would in the ground and need to be watered more frequently.

FACING PAGE, BOTTOM: Drip-irrigation systems simplify watering.

135

fertilizing

Start with a rich potting mix to give plant roots a healthy supply of nutrients.

Plants in containers live on limited resources. Initially, they nourish themselves by photosynthesizing through their foliage and absorbing nutrients through their roots. But over time, the nutrients in the soil will be depleted. To keep your plants thriving and productive, you'll need to replenish those nutrients by adding organic matter or manmade supplements.

TOP TO BOTTOM:
Rich organic fertilizers such as compost break down slowly, feeding plant roots longer. Liquid fertilizers provide a quick dose of nutrients. Powdered fertilizers mixed into the soil surface deliver nutrients each time the plant is watered.

TYPES OF FERTILIZERS

Organic vs. Inorganic

Organic fertilizers are derived from animal or plant products. Besides providing essential nutrients, they also improve soil structure. Because they take time to break down, they work at a slower pace than inorganic products and therefore last longer. Examples of good organic fertilizers are compost, some animal manures, fish emulsions, seaweed, and kelp.

Inorganic fertilizers are chemical additives derived from non-living materials. Their primary benefit is that they are fast acting. The nutrients are immediately available to plant roots for quick results.

Wet or Dry

Dry fertilizers come in powders, granules, or time-release capsules. Apply by spreading on the soil surface and then raking into the soil mix. The fertilizer is activated and dispersed each time you water.

Liquid fertilizers come in crystal, granule, or liquid concentrate form. After mixing with water, apply using a watering can or spray bottle. Some liquid formulations, known as foliar-feed fertilizers, provide immediate nutrients when sprayed directly on a plant's leaves.

ABOVE: Granular fertilizers mixed with soil provide a controlled-released feeding. One application can nourish a container garden for several weeks.

ABOVE RIGHT: Some plants benefit from the application of fertilizer directly to their foliage, also known as foliar feeding. Liquid fish emulsion and kelp are great organic fertilizers for foliar feeding.

A HEALTHY DIET

All plants need three major minerals to thrive and produce: **nitrogen** (N) stimulates green growth, **phosphorus** (P) promotes root development as well as flower and fruit production, and **potassium** (K) strengthens a plant's defenses against disease, drought, and cold temperatures. In addition to these three macronutrients, plants need small quantities of other minerals, known as micronutrients.

When buying fertilizer, you'll find a set of three numbers on the packaging (16-16-16, for example) that indicates the percentage of each macronutrient by weight. The first number represents nitrogen, the second is phosphorus, and the third represents potassium. For containers, it's generally best to use a fertilizer with equal or nearly equal amounts of the three macronutrients.

When you purchase a plant from a nursery, see if any fertilizing information is included on the label; if not, ask your nursery person for the recommended type and amount of fertilizer.

Below is a guide to troubleshooting nutrient deficiencies in your plants. If you notice any of these signs, remedy the problem by adding a fertilizer specifically formulated to be high in the deficient mineral.

RECOGNIZING NUTRIENT DEFICIENCIES

SYMPTOMS	DEFICIENCY
Yellow leaves that are smaller than normal; leaves may turn red or purple. Overall growth is stunted or dwarfed.	Nitrogen
Early leaf drop. Overall growth is reduced or weakened, flower and fruit production stops. Leaf margins may appear scorched, purple, or blue-green in color.	Phosphorus
Leaf tips and margins become yellow and scorched with brownish purple spotting underneath.	Potassium
Yellow between leaf veins. Foliage may turn completely yellow.	Iron
Leaf veins become reddish yellow and puckered; leaves eventually turn brown and die.	Magnesium
Leaf veins become light yellow and take on a netted appearance. Further stress gives the foliage a gray metallic sheen with dark freckled dead tissue appearing along the leaf veins.	Manganese
Entire plant turns yellow. Leaf veins turn reddish. Leaves become twisted and brittle.	Sulfur
Very small leaves that turn yellow. Leaf veins remain green but die where they begin to branch.	Zinc

Plants grown in containers need a healthy diet of nutrients to stimulate green growth, strong roots, disease resistance, and fruit and flower production.

Neatly pruned
boxwoods have
a formal,
sculptured look.

W hy prune? The primary reasons are the three Ds: damaged, diseased, or dead growth that needs to be removed. But there are plenty of other situations that call for judicious pruning. Here are some ways that pruning keeps plants in top form.

Rejuvenate a Leggy, Overextended Plant

Tip pruning—removing one-third to one-half of soft, new growth—will encourage a plant to become bushier and more compact. **Deadheading**—removing spent flowers and stems—is effective in stimulating plants to rebound with fresh growth.

Both techniques are great ways to keep annuals, herbaceous perennials, succulents, and other small-scale container plants full and lush.

Improve Air Circulation

For trees and shrubs grown in containers, **pruning out crossed or crowded branches** improves air circulation, decreasing the potential for fungal or insect infestation. The added benefit: It promotes good plant form.

Give Plants a Head Start

For trees, shrubs, or climbers, an **initial pruning and shaping at the time of planting** can set the stage for compact container growth. After your plant is situated in its container, prune weak shoots or stems down to the soil line and keep just a few strong shoots that have at least 2 or 3 buds. This process encourages stronger, lusher new growth. As the plant grows, shape it as you like.

Keep Plants within Bounds

Another method to control container growth for trees and certain shrubs is **root pruning**, best done in late autumn. If the roots appear to be overcrowded or the plant is looking too large for its container, extract it from the pot and check the root ball. Are the roots circling and twisting around themselves, taking up most of the pot? If so, they need trimming. Tease the circling roots out of the tangled mass, and use pruners or a pruning saw to remove a third to half of the root. Place the root ball back into the container and fill with fresh soil. Be sure to water as normal. Don't wait for signs of stress—you want the plant to think it's business as usual.

Remove "Reverting" Foliage

Many plants that have mottled, multicolored, or striped leaves owe their distinctive foliage to a mutation. Occasionally, these plants send out new growth that has reverted to its original solid green. If you're not happy with the way-ward foliage, the cure is simple: **Prune off the reverted shoots.** It won't harm the plant at all.

TOP: Deadheading, or removing spent flowers, helps promote repeat bloom.

BOTTOM: Occasional pruning is a good way to keep plants in containers at a healthy and appropriate size.

PRUNING 101

First and foremost, always prune with sharp, clean tools. Dull tools can cause ragged or torn cuts that create easy access for pests and disease. The smoother and cleaner the cut, the better it will heal.

It's a good practice to cut back to healthy tissue and prune just above points on stems where foliage emerges. For plants whose buds occur in an alternate or staggered arrangement, prune ⅛ inch above an outward-facing bud at a 45° angle. For plants whose buds occur opposite one another on a stem, prune ⅛ inch above both buds in a straight horizontal line.

When pruning diseased plants, sterilize your pruning tools after each cut to avoid spreading pests and/or disease to other plants. Use a solution of 1 part bleach mixed with 10 parts water.

To keep annuals looking lush and blooming throughout the season, tip prune and dead-head to encourage prolific compact growth and repeat blooming.

Prune perennials back by one-third to one-half after their initial bloom to encourage an encore production of flowers. As needed, cut back plants again at the end of their growing season to prepare them for healthy new growth the following year.

Climbing vines that flower early on old wood from the previous summer should be pruned right after flowering. For climbers that flower during spring and summer on new growth from the current season, prune in winter or early spring while the plant is dormant.

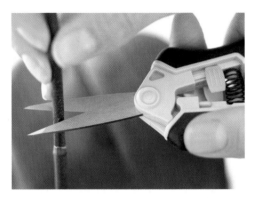

ABOVE: Clean, sharpened pruning tools foster healthy healing of pruning cuts, minimizing the spread of disease and fungal infection.

FACING PAGE: Providing a support structure for sprawling or vining plants reduces stem breakage. It also keeps fruit and flowers from lying in soil.

WHEN TO PRUNE TREES AND SHRUBS

TYPE OF PLANT	OPTIMAL PRUNING TIME
Fruit Trees	Depends on the species; find guidance at your nursery, in a pruning manual, or online
Deciduous Trees	Summer or winter
Conifers	Spring or summer
Spring-Flowering Shrubs	Right after flowering to encourage new growth and set the stage for future flowering
Summer-Flowering or Fruiting Shrubs	After flowering or fruiting, in late winter or early spring

TRAINING

So you've got a very happy plant that is feeling frisky and growing vigorously in its container. To keep your plant from flopping over, you need to give it some support. Twigs, bamboo canes, stakes, metal supports, or a small trellis will do the job.

For vines and creeping plants, create a tripod or "tipi" with stakes or canes. Twist your vines around these supports and gently tie with twine. As the plant grows, you may need to guide its growth occasionally and secure with additional ties.

care tips

» When using support structures, make sure the container is heavy and deep enough to support both the structure and the plant.

» For a contemporary look, use black or blue bamboo canes as supports. They retain their color and look very sculptural in the garden.

» Height of stakes should measure about two-thirds of the plant's height at maturity.

Fruit trees in containers can be trained to sprawl against a wall, producing a harvest in a limited space.

THE ART OF ESPALIER

If you have limited space and want a sophisticated way to showcase container trees or shrubs, consider training them to grow flat against a wall or vertical structure—a process known as *espalier*. This style of shaping is relatively simple to achieve, provided you do occasional maintenance and fine-tuning.

Dwarf fruit trees and shrubs are excellent candidates for espaliering. All you have to do is set up a trellis or wiring system within 8 to 12 inches of your container. As the plant grows, secure its branches in a fanlike or tiered fashion to the support. Follow the steps at right to create a formal espalier.

Creating an informal, organic-looking espalier is even easier. Choose plants that grow naturally in a horizontal or tiered form. Let them branch against your structure, clipping off only those shoots that stick out too far.

GOOD PLANTS FOR AN INFORMAL ESPALIER

» *Camellia*

» *Cercis*, **redbud**

» *Chaenomeles*, **quince**

» *Cotoneaster*

» *Duranta*, **sky flower**

» *Ficus carica*, **fig**

» *Fremontodendron*, **flannel bush**

» *Loropetalum*, **fringe flower**

» *Magnolia stellata*, **star magnolia**

» *Pyracantha*, **firethorn**

» *Viburnum*

❶ Remove Extraneous Branches

Choose two strong branches that grow laterally from the central trunk (leader) to form the first tier; remove all other shoots and cut back the central leader to just above the bottom tier of wire or support trellis beam. Bend branches to a 45° angle and secure them loosely to your support structure with jute or plastic ties. Over the first growing season, gradually tighten ties so that branches are horizontal by the end of the season.

❷ Tie Branches Horizontally

When a new central leader sprouts and becomes long enough, hold it upright and tie it to the second tier of your support system. During the first dormant season, cut back any new leader growth to the second tier. Now choose two branches from below for the second horizontal tier and remove any competing shoots. Cut lateral growth on the lower branches back to three buds.

❸ Tie a Second Tier of Branches

During the second growing season, gradually bring the second-tier branches into a horizontal position, as described in step 1. Keep the leader upright and tie it to the third tier. If you like, repeat the process in the following season for a fourth wire. When the leader reaches the top tier, cut it back to just above the top branch.

❹ Prune as Needed

Keep horizontal branches under control by pruning back the ends to downward facing side branches in late spring or summer. Also prune away any suckering sprouts that appear at the base of your plant—they can divert energy from the espaliered growth above.

repotting

If you're treating your plants right, they're going to thrive, and eventually they may need a larger home. If a plant looks crowded or out of proportion to its container, or if roots are creeping out the bottom, it's ready for roomier quarters. Repotting can also help a plant that is growing poorly but has no sign of pests or disease. Mature trees and shrubs should be repotted every 3 to 4 years. The best time to repot plants is in the spring or early summer.

HOW TO REPOT A PLANT

❶ Start with Fresh Soil

Select a new container that's an inch or two larger in diameter and depth than the current container. If your new container has been used previously, clean it with a stiff brush and a solution of 1 part bleach mixed with 10 parts water. Rinse thoroughly. Fill it about one-third with soil. Always use fresh soil to prevent the spread of possible pests and diseases.

❷ Remove Plant from Its Old Pot

If you can manage it, invert the container and support the top of soil with one hand. Use a slow, shaking motion to dislodge the plant. If the root ball is tight, try working a narrow trowel around the perimeter of the soil to dislodge it.

❸ Loosen the Root Ball

Examine the root ball. If you notice lots of dense nonfibrous roots circling around the root ball, cut them back by one-third. Gently tease the remaining roots out of the root ball and form into a loose bundle. If any roots are black or smelly, cut them out.

❹ Transfer to the New Pot

Make sure you place the plant in the new container at its original depth. Fill in with the new soil mix and press firmly but not too firmly.

❺ Water

Give your plant a thorough, gentle watering to help roots settle in.

FACING PAGE: For plants that have outgrown their container or are just not performing well, repotting is one method to help revive them.

HOW TO DIVIDE A PLANT

After several seasons in a container, many perennials need to be divided so they can rejuvenate. Dividing plants is also a great way to multiply your collection. Division should be done in early spring or autumn.

① Cut through the Root Ball

Remove plant from its container. With a sharp blade, root pruners, root saw, or trowel, carefully cut or slice through plant crown. If the plant is small and malleable enough, you can use your hands to gently pull it apart.

② Divide into Pieces

Using your hands, gently separate the plant and its root ball into two or more pieces. Keep vigorous outer growth and discard weak, old, or diseased growth.

③ Replant Each Division

Tease the roots of each root ball into a loose bundle. Fill your clean container half to two-thirds full of fresh soil to make a platform for your newly divided plant's roots. The level depends on how much new root ball needs to be accommodated, so adjust accordingly. Lower plant roots into your container so that the crown of the plant is about 1 inch below the rim.

④ Add More Soil

Fill in with fresh soil. Press soil firmly but not too firmly so that your new division is stable in its new home. Water gently but thoroughly.

FACING PAGE: Dividing plants and potting up additional containers is an inexpensive way to expand your container garden collection.

pests
and diseases

Slugs can polish off
plants quickly, so be
on the lookout.

Plants in container gardens are just as susceptible to pests and diseases as any other garden plant. The best way to manage harmful culprits is to identify them and act as soon as you can. The following pages identify common pests and diseases that can wreak havoc on your container gardens.

PESTS	CONTROLS

Aphids

These small soft-bodied insects are usually found on new growth and flower buds. They can be lime green, yellow, red, or black in color. Aphids damage plants by sucking out nutrient juices, causing curled yellow leaves and sometimes stunted growth. They secrete a substance that attracts ants; the presence of ants may indicate an aphid infestation.

Blast aphids off plants with a spray of water.

Crush them by hand.

Spray with insecticidal soap or horticultural oil such as neem.

Introduce ladybugs to the area of infestation.

Beetles and Weevils

These insects come in a variety of shapes and sizes. They chew holes in all parts of plants, sometimes transmitting disease in the process.

Handpick and drop into a bucket of hot soapy water.

Spray with insecticidal soap containing pyrethrin, derived from a plant in the chrysanthemum family, or horticultural oil such as neem.

Apply beneficial nematodes to soil. They can assist in killing beetle larvae.

Caterpillars

The larvae of many flying insects can ravage plants by chewing holes and consuming foliage, flowers, and fruit. One particular pest to watch out for is the larvae of the light brown apple moth. This caterpillar does not discriminate when it comes to eating plants and is slowly spreading from the West Coast eastward.

Spray with an organic pesticide that contains naturally occurring bacteria called *Bacillus thuringiensis* var. *kurstaki*, or BTK.

Apply Spinosad, a pesticide containing naturally occurring bacteria that controls a variety of insects.

Mealybugs

These soft-bodied, cottony white insects are sap-suckers. Like aphids, they secrete honeydew, attracting molds and other fungus to grow and fester. Other symptoms include yellow foliage, leaf drop, and premature fruit drop.

Spray with insecticidal soap or horticultural oil such as neem.

Treat infested areas with a 1-to-4 dilution of rubbing alcohol and water, applied with a spray bottle or a cotton swab. (First test a part of the plant that is not visible. Observe for 24 hours. If foliage is not affected, the solution is safe to use on the rest of the plant.)

Scale Insects

Scales are another type of sap-sucking insect. They can appear as waxy, bumpy, fuzzy growths on leaves and stems. Underneath these growths, the insect pierces through plant tissue to suck out nutrients. Heavy scale infestation can cause poor growth and possible dieback (the gradual dying of shoots starting at the tips).

Spray with horticultural oil such as neem.

Douse with a dilution of rubbing alcohol and water (see "Mealybugs").

NOTE: Insecticidal soaps are effective only on the mobile crawling stage of this insect.

continued on page 152

PESTS	CONTROLS

Slugs and Snails

Slugs and snails ravage plants by chewing large, ragged holes in stems, foliage, and flowers.

Fasten copper banding around containers to repel them.

Remove by hand.

Set out a tray of beer; snails will crawl in and drown.

Use iron phosphate pellets, which are nontoxic to pets and wildlife.

Spider Mites

Spider mites are tiny arachnids related to spiders and ticks. They are very small and can be difficult to spot. They attack plants by sucking out juices from the undersides of leaves, causing them to yellow and drop. Another sign of infestation is the abundance of spun webbing.

Spray with insecticidal soap or horticultural oil such as neem in early spring as a preventive.

Thrips

These tiny torpedo-shaped insects are almost invisible to the eye. They suck juices and chlorophyll from foliage, flowers, buds, and new growth. Signs of their destruction usually don't appear until after they have gone. Foliage on an affected plant will take on a bronze or silvery sheen due to the depletion of chlorophyll.

Spray with a dormant horticultural oil early in the season.

Spray with insecticidal soap throughout the growing season.

Whiteflies

Whiteflies are a pest of many garden plants, especially fruit trees and vegetables. They lay eggs on the undersides of leaves and grow into tiny mothlike insects with a powdery white coating. They like to suck plant nutrients from both new and old growth.

Spray with insecticidal soap or horticultural oil such as neem.

Hang or post sticky yellow whitefly traps, available at nurseries. The traps won't eliminate the pests completely, but can reduce their presence.

DISEASES	CONTROLS

Black Sooty Mold

Black sooty mold usually occurs when pests secrete honeydew on plants. The windblown spores of this mold stick to honeydew and grow. As the spores grow, a black mold develops that blocks light to plant surfaces and mars the appearance of the plant.

Wash mold off with a spray of water.

Control and eliminate any honeydew-producing pests that might be on the plant.

Spray affected areas with fungicides.

Leaf Spot

Many fungi and bacteria cause leaf spot. Once the fungus gets into the leaf, it multiplies—destroying leaf tissue and leaving a dark spot that can be the size of a pinhead or encompass the entire leaf. The damage is primarily cosmetic.

Remove all affected leaves.

Keep container free of affected leaf debris.

Avoid overhead watering.

Mosaic Virus

Symptoms of this virus include mottled or distorted foliage with yellow spots. Foliage curls up or appears stunted.

Remove or destroy affected areas or entire plant.

Sterilize tools and hands after contact with virus to avoid its spread.

Control and eliminate sap-sucking insects and beetles, which can spread the disease.

Powdery Mildew

This fungus first appears as round white spots that can merge into a dusting of grayish white powder on foliage and flowers. It occurs in conditions that promote excess humidity, such as plants spaced closely together, dense growth that stifles air circulation, and shade or fog.

Prune plants to create optimal air circulation.

Spray affected areas with fungicides.

Spray with a solution of 2 teaspoons baking soda and horticultural oil mixed with water.

Rust

Rust appears as small orange or dark brown spots on the undersides of plant foliage. As the spots grow, the fungus spreads and coats the foliage. It usually occurs in damp, humid situations.

Remove affected leaves, spray with fungicide.

Spray with a solution of 3 teaspoons baking soda and 1 teaspoon nondetergent dishwashing liquid or canola oil in 1 gallon of water.

Finishing the Look

Now you're ready to let your container garden shine. Where you locate it and how you display it are as much a part of the look as the combination of plants and pot you've so carefully put together. This section will give you pointers on placing containers for maximum impact, whether it's a single pot or an artfully arranged grouping. You'll also see examples of the many places container gardens can enliven with color, texture, and dimension—from rooftops to balconies, blank walls to entryways.

Identical containers placed at varying levels create a stunning backdrop for this seating area.

adding
impact

Bromeliads and other tropical container plantings edging the perimeter of a patio set an exotic mood.

To display your container garden to full effect, consider how it will serve as a design element. Just like throw pillows, rugs, or artwork, container gardens can be visual anchors that can define, organize, and connect spaces. These anchors give the eyes a place to rest. They grab attention and make you stop and take notice before moving on.

SETTING A MOOD

If you're striving for a formal atmosphere, choose similar containers and space them evenly. Use plants with strong shapes and keep them well manicured. If you prefer an informal feeling, mix things up and contrast the shapes of your containers and their plantings. Create vignettes where large containers are surrounded by smaller ones. And for a contemporary look, use an orderly placement, and choose bold plantings that focus on texture rather than color.

care tip

>> Be careful when placing tall containers with top-heavy plants. These compositions can become unbalanced and fall over easily, causing damage or injury. Try filling tall containers with low-growing or cascading plants instead—they will provide counterbalance and won't become top-heavy.

Chic painted urns on pedestals add a vertical element that gives this setting a relaxed, room-like quality.

A cluster of containers forms an island of interest, showcasing plants with striking form in a sea of glamorous tumbled glass.

PLANTINGS WITH PURPOSE

More than decoration, container gardens can serve multiple functions. They can put a garden in places where you otherwise couldn't grow anything. Their mobility and flexibility let you move them around to create lush garden beds, refresh spaces with a touch of green, or design focal points that draw the eye to what you think is truly special. They can magically transform an area with an artificial feel into a place of natural beauty.

ABOVE: With container gardens as the walls and an overhead canopy as the roof, this seating area becomes an intimate outdoor room.

ABOVE RIGHT: A wooden window box filled with geraniums transforms an empty space into a cheerful spot.

RIGHT: Rounded forms and living greenery soften the stark expanse of hard surfaces.

AN EYE FOR PLACEMENT

Take into account how and where your container garden will be observed. Will you view it through a window? Seated in a chair? Try standing or sitting in or near the space and see where your eyes go. If a particular spot draws your focus, more than likely, that's where others will look as well.

If what you see are blank walls, place container gardens that provide color and fine texture against them to make the area pop visually. Want to make narrow or small areas feel larger? Position your container garden at the far end to produce a sense of depth and visually elongate the space. If you have a symmetrical space with some room, put a container garden in the center to create a sense of flow and activate the space.

ABOVE: A raised pedestal container filled with *Kalanchoe pumila* becomes a focal point in the center of a space.

RIGHT: Massing containers holding succulents of different shapes and sizes multiplies their impact.

grouping

This grouping of container plantings creates an impromptu bed of interesting shapes, textures, and colors, infusing personality into a once-empty space.

Grouping container gardens is an impactful way to create a moment and cause a stir in a space dying for attention. When you group containers, the goal is to produce an attractive visual effect that is neither clunky nor confusing. As garden writer Thomas Hobbs says, "A grouping of containers should look like a gallery exhibit, not a garage sale."

VIBRANT VIGNETTES

One of the benefits of container gardening is that you can assemble the containers into a staging or vignette for full impact. You can use even- or odd-numbered combinations to create an engaging display. This works best when displaying container gardens in groups of 2 to 5.

Duo
2 CONTAINERS
Lay out diagonally for greatest impact.

Triangulated Trio
3 CONTAINERS
Lay out in a triangular pattern. This staggered look puts containers in active positions and creates a sense of flow. It also shows off line and shadow play among containers.

Diamond Formation
4 CONTAINERS
Lay out containers in a four-point diamond formation. For a casual look, don't stick to a rigid diamond layout—rotate the positioning a bit for a softer look.

ODD VS. EVEN

One of the most effective techniques for creating a successful grouping is with an odd number of containers. When you group elements in even pairs, their symmetry in close proximity can cause the eye to combine their presence and make them appear as only one element. On the other hand, groupings of 3, 5, 7, and so on, appear dynamic. They force the eye to move around, which provides a sense of visual separation, giving you more elements to observe.

The arrangement of three terra-cotta containers around an ornate fountain gives this vignette a classic, balanced look.

GROUPING BY SIZE

To ensure a cohesive design, avoid dramatic size discrepancies—don't pair a big container with a tiny one. They'll appear out of scale next to each other and leave you with an incomplete look. Instead, group containers that graduate from small to medium to large.

To create groupings with bold impact, give large containers the starring role and let the smaller ones act as the supporting cast. Place your larger containers in prominent positions either in the background or center of the grouping. This placement creates a sense of volume and depth that enlarges a space.

United by their richly textured surface, these containers of varying sizes create a dynamic display.

VARYING LEVELS

Elevating container gardens brings new excitement and dimension to areas short on space. It creates impact by reinforcing visual separation between the container and the ground. Elevation also adds interest by interrupting the flow of a space and drawing attention. Not only does a raised container garden spice things up visually, but it also lets you view plants differently. It's a method that gives plants a position of prominence. It increases their visibility when they might otherwise go unnoticed on the ground.

You can use a traditional plant stand to elevate your containers. Or seek out interesting alternatives: old sturdy tree stumps, sections of palm tree trunks, crates, concrete blocks, or even overturned empty containers. Just make sure all surfaces are level and that your choice of support structure is stable.

ABOVE: A modern container with a contemporary planting of Albany woollybush (*Adenanthos sericea*), *Sedum morganianum*, and rattail cactus (*Aporocactus flagelliformis*) is elevated in front of a concrete wall. Pots of cactus atop the wall add yet another level to the composition.

RIGHT: Raising a container to eye level is a great way to give it added visibility and encourage the enjoyment of its beauty.

163

outdoor living rooms

A simple wood deck becomes a livable outdoor room with the addition of a multitude of containers. They vary in size, shape, and level but share a common color palette, creating a harmonious scene.

Patios, decks, balconies, and rooftops should be thought of as "living rooms." These spaces provide places for entertaining, recreation, relaxation, and gardening. Unfurnished, these areas present hard surfaces that can be uninviting and far from natural. Container gardens are the perfect remedy to make these spaces truly livable. Their placement can turn a stark spot into a welcoming home.

PATIOS AND DECKS

Container gardens can serve multiple purposes on a patio or deck. As a design element, they have the power to soften the visual impact of areas where hard surfaces dominate. Use container gardens with lush foliage and bold flowers to enhance the color, texture, and form of a space.

Container gardens also offer a great way to outfit a patio or deck with boundaries, partitions, and backdrops. Use these elements to create enclosed intimate settings or "rooms" that provide you with additional places to relax and seek refuge all within one larger space.

TOP: Use container gardens of beautifully arranged foliage and flowers to soften the hard surfaces of a space and make them more inviting.

ABOVE: Groupings of containers provide vibrant living borders around this patio, extending down the steps and connecting to the garden.

BALCONIES

Balconies are extensions of your interior living space. They provide an intimate escape from the inside of your home where you can experience the outdoors. And, from the interior, they serve as a viewing gallery. Container gardens can enhance these spaces by providing visual interest, protection from the elements, and privacy.

One of the most important things to consider when placing a container garden on a balcony is whether or not the structure can support the weight. A container filled with soil and plants can become extremely heavy when watered. One way to reduce weight is to use lightweight containers with "soil-less" mixes. Another important precaution is to make sure the container is secure and will not topple over, causing possible damage or injury. Make sure railings are sturdy and that the hardware you use to affix containers is strong enough to hold them.

Balconies can be short on space. To preserve as much room as possible, choose containers that are narrow, rectangular, or have flat backs so that they can hug walls. Place your containers along the perimeter of your balcony to make the space feel bigger and longer.

One other thing to consider is exposure. Balconies raise container gardens up and out into the open where they are fully exposed to the elements. For a successful garden, choose drought- and wind-tolerant plants. Although a location like this can at times be harsh for plantings, with routine maintenance, balconies can provide a wonderful setting.

Symmetry and form are the stars of this chic arrangement of well-clipped boxwood shrubs and aesthetically pruned Japanese maples.

The narrow profile of this wooden container creates the illusion of a bigger, bolder space.

LEFT: Tough, drought-tolerant olive trees give these rooftop containers an elegant style set against the backdrop of an open sky.

BELOW: Rounded boxwood shrubs put on a playful display in contemporary containers and help define this inviting rooftop space.

FACING PAGE: Deep, densely planted containers create an intimate setting with a natural look. Besides their aesthetic appeal, they help buffer the rooftop seating area from the elements.

ROOFTOPS

Think of a rooftop space as a room without a ceiling, a great opportunity for taking advantage of the open sky overhead. An accessible rooftop space can be transformed into a garden room for entertaining or simply for getting outside.

As with balconies, it's important to determine whether a rooftop can support the added weight of container gardens. Stable and secure synthetic or metal containers that are lightweight provide the perfect solution. Also, use a lightweight "soil-less" mix when planting. Place your containers over rooftop support structures such as load-bearing walls or ceiling joists.

When it comes to planting your containers, consider that an open rooftop is exposed to extreme wind conditions and higher levels of light. Use resilient, drought-tolerant plants that are tough enough to stand up to the elements. Plants that need extra protection should be placed up against structures on your rooftop. Another way to provide protection from the elements is to group containers planted with tall, vertical, durable plants and shrubs. Not only will they create windbreaks, but they can also provide privacy and a safety barrier.

GOOD ROOFTOP PLANTS

» *Acacia*	» *Griselinia*
» *Agave*	» *Lomandra*
» *Banksia*	» *Murraya paniculata*
» *Buxus*	
» *Cedrus atlantica 'Glauca'*	» *Podocarpus*
	» *Senecio*
» *Coprosma*	» *Yew (Taxus)*
» *Cordyline*	» *Yucca*
» *Dudleya*	

in the garden

A blue container placed in the distance acts as an intriguing focal point that beckons you to come closer and discover the garden along the way.

Placing your containers in the garden is a great way to enliven dull areas, create contrast, and provide additional structure as well as framework. Use them as your garden's doors and windows. As doors, situate groupings of containers to indicate a transition from one part of your garden to the next. As windows, place containers to frame viewpoints or highlight an intended focal point.

To add punch to the landscape, inject container gardens in and around subtle flower beds or against solid backgrounds such as the wall of a freestanding structure. Experiment with placement and see what looks right.

NEAR OR FAR

In larger spaces, big containers are well suited to be out in the garden, away from the house. Use them as focal points to create areas of special interest. Their size and presence can draw the eye quickly to locations and encourage visitors to venture beyond the back door or patio—giving your garden an extended, spacious feeling.

Small containers look better close to home. When set out in the distance, they tend to get lost. Instead, place them filled with plants in attractive clusters close to the house, where they gain presence while bringing the look of the garden closer to the back door. Or if you want to include small containers at a distance, make them noticeable by elevating them to give them some presence. Both of these methods unify house and garden, creating a sense of spaciousness.

The scale of this aquatic container garden and its placement on a raised terrace command your attention and entice you to step up and see what it holds.

walls

Training climbers to scale a wall or an attractive vertical support not only saves space, but also creates a striking display as plants explore new horizons.

An empty wall can appear hard, cold, and unpleasant to the eye. However, that's great news for establishing a container garden—it presents you with a blank canvas, ripe for dressing up with something interesting placed at eye level. A container garden set against a wall can soften hard edges, create a sense of comfort, and reduce the feeling of confinement.

CONSIDER EXPOSURE

When placing container gardens against a wall or vertical surface, first think about what kind of exposure the site receives and for how long. Then choose plants that will thrive in those conditions. Plants that require full sun should get six or more hours of direct sunlight each day. If your site gets two to five hours of sun per day, opt for plants that do best in part shade.

RIGHT: Mount containers in a stable location that can support their weight, even when watered.

BELOW: A built-in container brings a wall to life with a bounty of fanciful foliage and soft, spilling form.

CLIMBING OR SPILLING

There are two container garden options that work well for walls and vertical spaces. One is to simply plant climbers in containers that can sit at the base of a wall. Use containers such as troughs or wooden wine barrels and provide your climbing plants with the support of a trellis or cabling. The other option is to use a wall-mounted container such as a wire basket, troughs with support brackets, or the latest in vertical gardening systems such as Woolly Pockets (see page 126).

CLIMBERS FOR CONTAINERS

» **Bougainvillea**

» **Bower vine (Pandorea jasminoides)**

» **Clematis**

» **Cup-and-saucer vine (Cobaea scandens)**

» **Honeysuckle (Lonicera)**

» **Passiflora**

» **Potato vine (Solanum jasminoides)**

» **Silvervein creeper (Parthenocissus henryana)**

» **Sweet pea (Lathyrus odoratus)**

THE NEW VERTICAL GARDEN

Innovative containers and planting systems are expanding the horizons of vertical gardening beyond the traditional wall-hanging planter. Gardens can assume a more vertical position with thin-profiled modular systems or fiber-walled containers. These containers sit more flush on vertical surfaces and allow the plants to be the star of the show. The units are designed to be used individually or linked together to form a vertical tapestry of living plants. You can hang your vertical garden anywhere there is a wall that can bear the load.

Water your vertical garden when soil approaches dryness, about every 7 to 10 days. To water, remove the frame from the wall, lay it flat, water lightly, and let the soil drain before hanging up again. The steps below show you how to build and plant a vertical garden.

① Start with a Frame

Purchase a vertical garden frame or build one with wood sides, ½-inch hardware wire mesh, and a plywood back.

② Gather Cuttings

Break off small pieces from succulents you already have; the stems should be at least ¼ inch long. For a 6- by 12-inch frame, you'll need about 60 cuttings. Set them aside in a cool area for a few days to allow the stem ends to dry and callus over.

③ Add Soil

Set the frame mesh side up on a flat surface; fill it with moist cactus mix, working the mix through the mesh with your fingers. The mesh and the wood backing will hold the soil in place.

④ Plant Cuttings

Poke the stem ends through the mesh and into the soil. Leave the frame lying flat in a cool, bright location while cuttings take root, about 7 to 10 days, then begin watering. Once plants are securely rooted—which takes between 4 and 12 weeks—display the frames upright in an area that gets morning or filtered sun.

A mosaic of sculptural succulents forms a living work of art with contemporary flair.

hanging
containers

A brick wall makes a richly textured backdrop for a hanging pot of Spanish lavender.

H anging containers draw attention to spaces that might otherwise be a void. Plants bring a relaxed, nurturing feeling to these areas.

PLACEMENT POINTERS

To create the best view, hang container gardens against hard surfaces or solid backdrops. Fill them with plants that cascade or extend over their rims. A spilling look provides a pleasing visual energy that can make your hanging container garden a feast for the eyes. Use lots of texture too.

Strategic placement of a hanging container can block an undesirable view or create a bit of privacy. Just be sure to hang containers where no one will bump into them.

HOW TO HANG YOUR GARDEN

Make sure that the wall or overhead area where you attach your container can support its weight when watered. Use plant hangers or brackets made of wrought iron, wire, or steel that won't rust and will provide adequate support. Dark-colored hangers, which tend to disappear into the background, create the illusion that your container is floating. Light-colored hangers and wires are much more visible and can result in a clunky or tangled look.

To give your container garden plenty of clearance and room to grow, it's best if you can find a bracket that extends from the wall twice as far as the container's diameter. Hangers with swivel hooks—available at hardware stores as well as online—allow you to easily rotate your container so that it can receive light on all sides and grow evenly. This eliminates the need to take your container down to turn it and then hang it again.

ABOVE RIGHT: The staggered placement of these hanging containers fills a visual void with fresh green foliage.

RIGHT: A decorative support bracket complements the enchanting look of a hanging container filled with the airy foliage of a fern.

window boxes

Windows provide a visual escape for those inside while also drawing curiosity from the world outside. Use container gardens in these locations to bring life and color to hard surfaces without taking up valuable floor space.

STAYING SECURE

If your windowsills are wide enough, you can simply place your container on them for an instant garden. Otherwise, affix your container securely with brackets or straps—remember that a window box will be heavy when it's planted. Also be sure to leave some space for air to circulate between the box and the wall of your house.

Of course, not all window boxes need to be elevated. If the bottom edge of your windows is low, just set your container garden on the ground.

FRAGRANT PLANTS FOR WINDOW BOXES

» **Chocolate cosmos** *(Cosmos astrosanguineus)*

» **Common heliotrope** *(Heliotropium arborescens)*

» **English lavender** *(Lavandula angustifolia)*

» *Freesia*

» *Hosta plantaginea* **'Aphrodite'**

» **Mint** *(Mentha)*

» **Pink** *(Dianthus)*

» **Scented geranium** *(Pelargonium)*

» **Shining jasmine** *(Jasminum laurifolium nitidum)*

» **Stock** *(Matthiola incana)*

» **Sweet alyssum** *(Lobularia maritima)*

» **Thyme** *(Thymus)*

Grow herbs or other fragrant plants in a window box where their scent can be enjoyed indoors.

design tip

» For a formal look, keep plant placement identical in each window box. For an informal look, use the same plants in each container, but shift their placement from one to the next.

Richly hued containers filled with vibrant plantings relate to the spicy color of the front door to create a bold, welcoming impact.

ontainer gardens at an entry set the mood for the space beyond even before people step inside. They can serve as beacons of color, texture, and form that tempt the viewer to come closer and help them feel welcome as they pass by. The element of nature that container gardens provide can make the transition from the exterior world to the interior (and vice versa) a relaxing one. Remember, you're creating a first and lasting impression. So go for impact and draw some attention.

ABOVE: The contemplative quality of containers filled with bamboo and *Cedrus atlantica* 'Glauca Pendula' hint at a calm, soothing atmosphere beyond these doors.

TOP RIGHT: Classic containers filled with neatly pruned roses frame the entry of an English-style garden and introduce a formal ambience.

RIGHT: Flanking the entry of a lush garden, containers filled with the tropical foliage of phormium set the scene as they transport you to a garden paradise.

A bold and bright display of bougainvillea in containers creates an attractive boundary and beautiful safety barrier for a stairway without a railing.

S tairs and walkways serve as links between spaces. Container gardens not only spruce up these locations with some style and color, but they can also provide a sense of guidance, signaling transition and direction.

SMART AND SAFE

Container gardens for stairways and paths should be bold and architectural to draw attention and indicate their presence. Multiples of the same pot evenly spaced will further emphasize the flow of traffic.

Use durable containers and sturdy plants because they're likely to be brushed against as people pass. Be conscious of the width of pathways and allow for safe passage.

For safety on stairs, stick with low-growing plants that won't obstruct the pathway. Also make sure that containers are either secured with straps to railings or fixed to surfaces, so they won't tumble and become a tripping hazard.

ABOVE: A collection of terra-cotta pots leads the eye, suggests flow, and signals a change in level.

RIGHT: Steps provide an excellent way to display an eclectic cluster of containers. The different levels create a layered look that shows off not only the plants but also their containers.

resource guide

All resources listed here offer online shopping and mail order. Some have catalogs as well.

Containers, Tools, and Other Supplies

Ace Hardware
www.acehardware.com
866-290-5334
Containers, tools, watering equipment, and other gardening supplies

Bauer Pottery
www.bauerpottery.com
888-213-0800
Selection of garden pottery

Ecoforms
www.ecoforms.com
707-823-1577
Manufacturer of Eco Pots, made from renewable and sustainable plant by-products

Felco
www.felco.com
High-quality Swiss-made garden tools

Fiskars
www.fiskars.com
866-348-5661
Gardening shears, watering cans, plant risers, and window box support brackets

Garden.com
www.garden.com
888-314-2733
Planters, tools, aquatic-garden supplies

Gardener's Supply Company
www.gardeners.com
888-833-1412
Selection of garden tools, irrigation, watering, pest control, and other garden supplies.

Hable Construction
www.hableconstruction.com
718-834-1752
Cotton canvas garden gloves

The Home Depot
www.homedepot.com
Containers, tools, and other gardening supplies

Ikea
www.ikea.com
Selection of affordable containers

Jamali Floral and Garden Supplies
www.jamaligarden.com
212-996-5534
Affordable garden pots

Lee Valley
www.leevalley.com
Containers, tools, and other garden supplies

Lowe's Home Improvement
www.lowes.com
Containers, tools, and other gardening supplies

Maison Reve
www.maisonreve.com
415-383-9700
Vintage urns, garden tools, and accessories from France

Modern Planter
www.modernplanter.com
800-563-0593
Contemporary containers

Paxton Gate
www.paxtongate.com
415-824-1872
Selection of pottery, plants, and other garden supplies

PlantContainers.com
www.plantcontainers.com
866-342-3330
Broad selection of containers

Planterixchange
www.planterixchange.com
800-448-2870
Broad selection of containers

The Plant Stand Company
www.eskimo.com/~bobg/index.html
800-834-9317
Makers of the Down Under Plant Stand; also sell pot sealer

Potted
www.pottedstore.com
323-665-3801
Unique containers

Pottery Barn
www.potterybarn.com
888-779-5176
Eclectic selection of containers

Radius Garden
www.radiusgarden.com
Ergonomic garden tools

SimplyPlanters.com
www.simplyplanters.com
866-579-5182
Broad selection of containers

Sprout Home
www.sprouthome.com
312-226-5950
718-388-4440
Contemporary containers

Target
www.target.com
Containers, tools, and some garden supplies; will feature Smith & Hawken garden products beginning in 2011

Terrain
www.shopterrain.com
877-583-7724
Unique containers and garden tools

Decorative Top Dressing

American Specialty Glass
www.americanspecialtyglass.com
877-294-4222
Wide selection of decorative tumbled glass (see Landscape/Store category on website)

Red Shovel Glass Co.
c/o Building Resources
www.buildingresources.org
415-285-7814
Wide selection of decorative tumbled glass, terra-cotta, and tile (select Tumbled Glass link)

Drip-Irrigation Supplies

Drip Depot
www.dripdepot.com
888-525-8874

Ewing Irrigation
www.ewing1.com
800-343-9464

Pest-Control Products, Organic Fertilizers, and Composting Supplies

Composters.com
www.composters.com
877-204-7336
Compost bins and composting supplies

Planet Natural
www.planetnatural.com
800-289-6656
Organic fertilizers, pest-control products, and other supplies

Safer Brand
www.saferbrand.com
800-800-1819
Organic pest-control products

Plants

Australian Native Plants Nursery
www.australianplants.com
800-701-6517
Protea and other Mediterranean-climate plants from Australia and South Africa

California Carnivores
www.californiacarnivores.com
707-824-0433
Carnivorous plants

Four Winds Growers
www.fourwindsgrowers.com
Dwarf citrus trees

Plant Delights Nursery
www.plantdelights.com
919-772-4794
Perennials, grasses, and agave

Pondplants.com
www.pondplants.com
800-578-5459
Water plants

Rainforest Flora
www.rainforestflora.com
310-370-8044
Air plants and bromeliads

White Flower Farm
www.whiteflowerfarm.com
800-503-9624
Wide selection of plants and bulbs, as well as tools, fertilizer, and pest-control supplies

YuccaDo
www.yuccado.com
979-542-8811
Drought- and heat-tolerant plants

Vertical Garden Supplies

Flora Grubb Gardens
www.floragrubb.com
415-626-7256
DIY vertical garden panels and the Woolly Pocket

Woolly Pocket
www.woollypocket.com
877-796-6559
Makers of the Woolly Pocket vertical and breathable garden

glossary

Acid-loving plants Plants that grow and thrive in soil with a low pH (below 7).

Air plant A type of plant that absorbs water and nutrients through its leaves, requiring no soil; also known as tillandsia.

Annual A plant that completes its life cycle in one growing season.

Aquatic plants Plants that grow with their roots on or under the water's surface.

Bright light A condition in which no direct sun reaches the area, but nothing is blocking the open sky.

Bulb An underground stem base that holds an embryonic plant surrounded by tissue that develops into leaves.

Chlorosis A yellowing of leaves, primarily due to an iron deficiency.

Compost Decaying organic matter that is used as a soil supplement and natural fertilizer.

Crown The point at which a plant's roots join its stem(s).

Cubic foot The volume of a cube that measures 1 foot on all sides.

Deadhead To remove spent (dead) flowers and stems.

Deciduous plants Those that shed their foliage at the end of a growing season. After a period of dormancy, leaves re-emerge.

Dense shade Areas that receive no sunlight but are still illuminated by dim ambient light.

Drip irrigation A method of irrigation that conserves water by delivering it slowly to the root zone of plants via micro-tubing and small emitters.

Espalier A technique of training plants to grow flat against a wall or vertical structure.

Evergreen plants Those that retain their leaves longer than one growing season.

Filtered light A situation in which sunlight is filtered through a canopy of tree leaves or a structure such as an arbor.

Full sun Six or more hours of direct sunlight per day.

Habit The overall growth pattern of a plant, such as upright, trailing, or columnar.

Hardiness A plant's ability to tolerate cold temperatures.

Horticultural oil A nontoxic, oil-based pesticide that eliminates insects primarily through suffocation.

Hybrid A plant whose parents are of two different species, subspecies, varieties, strains, or any combination thereof. Hybrid names are written with the symbol x, as in *Pelargonium* x *hortorum* 'Mrs. Pollock'.

Indirect light Bright, ambient light.

Leader The central, upward-growing stem of a single-trunked tree or shrub.

Leggy Describes plant growth that is spindly and weak.

Macronutrients Nutrients that plants need in large amounts: nitrogen (N), phosphorus (P), and potassium (K).

Micronutrients Nutrients that are essential to plants but are required in small amounts, such as zinc, iron, and copper.

Moisture gauge Device that measures the moisture content of soil.

Mulch A protective covering placed around plants that can prevent evaporation of moisture, insulate plant roots, deter the growth of weeds, or serve as a decorative accent.

Neem oil A natural insect repellent that comes from the oil pressed from the seeds and fruit of the evergreen neem tree (*Azadirachta indica*).

Organic matter Agricultural or gardening material derived from the natural products of living organisms.

Part sun/part shade Two to five hours of direct sunlight per day.

Perennial A plant that lives for three or more years.

Pot feet Structural devices used to elevate a pot to aid drainage and air circulation, as well as to avoid damaging contact between the pot and a surface.

Pot sealer A liquid used to coat pottery to prevent it from absorbing water and wicking moisture away from soil.

Pumice A form of volcanic rock used to provide additional drainage to soil or as a decorative mulch.

Silhouette A plant's basic outline, such as the naked form of a bare tree in winter.

Soil-less planting mix A light-weight planting mix that contains no soil. It is usually a combination of ingredients such as peat moss or coconut coir, tree bark, compost, pumice, and perlite.

Soil pH A measure of the soil's acidity or alkalinity. The pH scale ranges from 0 (extremely acidic) to 14 (extremely alkaline); a pH of 7 is neutral.

Soil polymer Granular, crystal, or gel-like additive; when mixed with soil, it has the ability to store water and nutrients, keeping them readily available for plant roots.

Species A subdivision of genus referring to groups of closely related plants with only minor differences.

Structure The shape of a plant, including the details of its foliage, stems, and flowers combined.

Succulent Fleshy plants with water-retaining leaves and structures, native to arid climates.

Sucker A vigorous shoot emerging from below the bud union on a grafted or budded plant, or any vertical shoot that grows from the trunk or horizontal branches.

Tender Describes plants that are intolerant of cold temperatures.

Texture The appearance or feel of a surface.

Top dressing Mulch that serves as a decorative or protective element placed around plants.

Training Guiding a plant so it will take on a desired shape.

Variety A natural or cultivated variant of a species. Cultivated varieties (cultivars) may be hybrids or selected varieties of plants that occur in the wild.

Vignette A self-contained decorative display of design elements.

Visual weight A property of color; the degree to which it catches the eye.

photography credits

Maxine Adcock/Photolibrary: 137 bottom left; **Sarl Akene/Photolibrary:** 70 bottom right; **Peter Anderson/Getty Images:** 131 bottom left bottom; **Red Cover/ Steve Back:** 169 top; **Michael Baumgarten:** 40 (published in *Bloom* magazine n°2), 50 left (published in *Bloom* magazine n°4); **BBC Magazines Ltd/GAP Photos:** 61; **Leigh Beisch:** 1 (design: Hank Jenkins, Lushland Design, www. lushlanddesign.com; styling: Philippine Scali; container from Pottery and Beyond, www.potsby.com; outdoor pillows by Hable Construction, www.hableconstruction.com),

64–65 (styling: Philippine Scali; garden belt and gardening gloves by Hable Construction, www.hable construction.com), 68 top left, 68 bottom left, 69 (styling: Philippine Scali; spool from Maison Reve, www.maisonreve.com), 70 top right, 70 bottom left, 72 (design: Hank Jenkins, Lushland Design, www.lushlanddesign.com; styling: Philippine Scali; containers from Potted L.A. www.pottedstore.com), 73 top left, 73 top right, 73 bottom, 74 (design: Hank Jenkins, Lushland Design, www.lushlanddesign.com; styling: Philippine Scali; props from Maison Reve, www.maisonreve.

com; container from Pottery and Beyond, www.potsby.com), 75 top, 75 bottom, 79, 80 (design: Hank Jenkins, Lushland Design, www. lushlanddesign.com; styling: Philippine Scali; containers from Pottery and Beyond, www.potsby.com), 81 left, 81 right, 82 (design: Hank Jenkins, Lushland Design, www. lushlanddesign.com; styling: Philippine Scali; container from Pottery and Beyond, www.potsby.com; outdoor pillows by Hable Construction, www.hableconstruction.com), 86 (design: Hank Jenkins, Lushland Design, www.lushlanddesign.com; styling: Philippine Scali; container

from Flora Grubb Garden, www. floragrubb.com; props from Maison Reve, www.maisonreve.com), 87 top left, 87 top right, 87 bottom, 88 (design: Hank Jenkins, Lushland Design, www.lushlanddesign.com; styling: Philippine Scali; containers from Bauer Pottery, www.bauer pottery.com; props from Maison Reve, www.maisonreve.com), 89, 90 (design: Hank Jenkins, Lushland Design, www.lushlanddesign.com; styling: Philippine Scali; containers from Potted L.A., www.pottedstore. com), 91 top, 91 bottom, 92 (design: Hank Jenkins, Lushland Design, www.lushlanddesign.com; styling: Philippine Scali; container from Flora Grubb Gardens, www. floragrubb.com), 93 top, 93 bottom, 99, 100 (design: Hank Jenkins, Lushland Design, www.lushland design.com; styling: Philippine Scali; containers from Bauer Pottery, www.bauerpottery.com), 101 top, 101 bottom, 102 (design: Hank Jenkins, Lushland Design, www.lushlanddesign.com; styling: Philippine Scali; container from Flora Grubb Gardens, www.flora grubb.com), 105, 107 top, 107 bottom, 110 (design: Jared Crawford/ Altar Ecos, www.altar-ecos.com; styling: Philippine Scali), 111 top, 111 bottom, 112 (design: Hank Jenkins, Lushland Design, www. lushlanddesign.com; styling: Philippine Scali; container from Potted L.A., www.pottedstore.com), 113, 120 (design: Hank Jenkins, Lushland Design, www.lushland design.com; styling: Philippine Scali; container from Potted L.A., www.pottedstore.com), 122 (design: Hank Jenkins, Lushland Design, www.lushlanddesign.com; styling: Philippine Scali; containers from Bauer Pottery, www.bauer pottery.com), 123 top, 124 (design: Hank Jenkins, Lushland Design, www.lushlanddesign.com; styling: Philippine Scali; container from Pottery and Beyond, www.potsby. com), 125, 131 top row center, 131 bottom left, back cover top (design: Jared Crawford/Altar Ecos, www.

index